The Baking Cookbook for Teens

The BAKING COOKBOOK *for* TEENS

75 DELICIOUS RECIPES FOR SWEET & SAVORY TREATS

Robin Donovan

PHOTOGRAPHY BY MARIJA VIDAL

ROCKRIDGE PRESS

Designer: Katy Brown
Editor: Pippa White
Production Editor: Erum Khan
Photography © Marija Vidal, 2018; food styling by Cregg Green
Illustrations © Yevhenia Haidamaka, 2018

ISBN: Print 978-1-64152-137-6 | eBook 978-1-64152-138-3

For Cashel, my favorite young baker

CONTENTS

INTRODUCTION

Welcome, new bakers! I had a serious sweet tooth as a kid, which is why I started baking at a pretty young age. As soon as I was old enough to use the electric mixer and stove on my own, you can bet the first thing I did was start whipping up sweet treats any time my mom would let me. I found that baking satisfied something in me that went beyond appetite—it became a creative outlet, a way for me to show my love for family and friends, a way to honor and celebrate people I cared about on special occasions, and quite honestly, a way to impress people. Also, it was lots of fun.

By the time I hit my teens, I was hungry for more recipes and more knowledge about baking in general. But at that time there were no baking books for someone my age, no guides to help me find my way through the world of baking or understand the language. So I did what any teen who was dying for cookies would do: I pored over my mother's baking books looking for the simplest recipes I could find, those that a) didn't have too many ingredients, b) didn't have any ingredients I wasn't familiar with, and c) didn't use any equipment I didn't recognize. If a recipe called for something I'd never heard of, I just skipped over it. Fortunately, that left plenty of options—lots of baking recipes use very basic ingredients and equipment—but it didn't help me learn or stretch my abilities.

This is the book I wish I'd had. Part 1 provides a rundown on basic baking techniques, ingredients, terminology, and equipment. Read through this section first. Or go straight to the recipes and dive in, knowing that the information is there for you when you need it.

Parts 2 and 3 of the book are where the fun really begins—the recipes! The book includes more than 75 recipes for all sorts of baked goods. There are chapters on breakfast treats and desserts (like cookies, brownies, bars, cakes, cupcakes, pies, and more!). Plus there are chapters on salty breads and snacks, pizza, savory tarts, and easy dinners.

If you haven't already discovered how much fun baking can be, you'll quickly learn it here. Soon you'll be baking treats to satisfy all of your deepest cravings, and you'll also look like a rock star to your friends and family as you wow them with your new skills. There's even an index in the back of the book that you can turn to when you want to make something to bring to a bake sale, study session, pep rally, birthday party, or any other occasion you can think of.

The recipes here range from easy—like basic drop cookies—to more challenging, like an apple pie with streusel topping. The idea is to start with recipes that you can make with little or no experience, and then build on your skills and keep gaining confidence as a baker. Begin with the easier recipes (labeled as Level 1), and as you develop more ability and comfort in the kitchen, move on to more challenging treats (Levels 2 and 3). And remember, you can always circle back to part 1 of the book to brush up on techniques or terms as you go.

I'm sure you're just as eager to get started as I am, so grab your apron and let's head to the kitchen!

Mastering

the Kitchen

PART ONE

The BASICS of BAKING

You're probably ready to jump in and start baking, and believe me, we will! But first, let's tackle a few basics that will help you succeed every time you bake—things like the difference between baking and cooking, how to prep like a pro, how to set up your work station and use common kitchen tools, cleanup, safety, and key words you'll want to know before you turn on the oven.

BAKING VS. COOKING

I know what you're thinking: Isn't baking a type of cooking? It is, but there are very different skills involved in baking as opposed to more general cooking. Both involve combining edible ingredients, chopping, mixing, and using heat to finish, but baking requires much more precision than cooking.

While many people cook by following recipes to a tee, the process of cooking is much more forgiving than baking. An experienced cook can improvise just about every step of the process, eyeballing measurements, testing doneness by sight or touch, and seasoning as they go. Recipes may instruct you to "add a handful of raisins," "stir occasionally," or "season to taste." In cooking, making substitutions on the fly is no big deal. If you're out of lemons, just use lime juice. Out of white sugar? Use brown. No onions in the pantry? Go ahead and substitute scallions or leeks. And so on.

Baking, on the other hand, is a more exacting science. Precise measurements, cooking times and temperatures, and doneness cues (signs that your baked goods are done) can spell the difference between success and failure in baking. Substitutions can be trickier—if you run out of baking powder, for instance, you can't just use baking soda instead.

IT'S ALL ABOUT FLOUR

Baking recipes, in general, rely heavily on five categories of ingredients:

» **Fat:** Butter, vegetable shortening, oil, cream, cheese

» **Flavoring ingredients:** Chocolate, fruit, vanilla (and other flavored) extract, spices like cinnamon, ginger, and nutmeg

» **Flours:** Wheat flours (all-purpose flour, bread flour, pastry flour, cake flour) as well as wheat-free flours like rice flour or almond flour

» **Leaveners (things that make baked goods rise):** Baking powder, baking soda, eggs, yeast

» **Sweeteners:** Granulated sugar, brown sugar, confectioners' (or powdered) sugar, molasses, honey, maple syrup

A BAKER'S DOZEN

What's better than a dozen cupcakes? How about 13 cupcakes? This is known as a "baker's dozen."

If you order a dozen eggs, you'll get 12. Same thing if you ask the butcher for a dozen steaks or if you buy a pack of a dozen socks from the department store. But walk into a bakery and order a dozen of anything—bread rolls, cookies, cupcakes, donuts, or tartlets—and it's very likely you'll walk out happily with 13 of whatever delicious item you've purchased.

There are several theories for how this practice of throwing in a bonus evolved, but the most widely accepted explanation is that back in medieval England, the law stated that the price of bread was tied to the price of the wheat used to make it. Selling undersized loaves was a punishable offense, so bakers began the practice of tossing in a bit extra to be sure they weren't shorting anyone.

Of these ingredients, flour is the one most commonly associated with all sorts of baking—sweet or not. Almost every baking recipe contains some type of flour. This goes for cookies, bars, brownies, cakes, cupcakes, breads, and pastry crusts. They all begin with flour, which gives baked goods their foundation.

When I talk about flour, I mean wheat flour unless otherwise specified. All-purpose flour is a type of wheat flour that has a moderate level of protein. It's called "all-purpose" because it can be used successfully for most baked goods. Bread flour is ideal for making bread because it is higher in protein and develops the highest levels of gluten, the substance that gives bread its chewy structure. Flours with lower protein, like pastry flour or the even lower-protein cake flour, are ideal for recipes where you want a light, airy structure, such as cakes and pastry crusts. All-purpose flour falls between bread flour and pastry flour on the protein spectrum and can generally be substituted for either in a pinch. Occasionally, although not in this book, recipes will call for flours other than wheat—such as rice or almond flour. These wheat-free flours will be specified as such in the ingredient list.

PREP (AND CLEAN UP) LIKE A PRO

The pros do a thing they call *mise en place* (pronounced meez-un-plass). That's a French term that means to put everything in its place, or to set up everything you need to cook your recipe. It is important to have all the pieces in place before you begin so you don't leave out an ingredient or forget to grease a pan. You don't want to make the dough for chocolate chip cookies only to find you don't have any chocolate chips, right? Here are the basic things you need to do before you start baking—and after you're done:

Carefully Read the Recipe

Read the recipe all the way through. It is absolutely essential that you read the entire thing from start to finish at least once before you begin. This will prepare you to follow all the steps correctly as you go.

How many servings does the recipe make? This refers to how many people you are baking for. If you are making something for your family of four, but the recipe only makes 2 servings, you will need to double that recipe to get 4 servings.

Baking time. Check how long the dish needs to bake and also look for any timed steps that need to be taken into consideration. For instance, many yeasted breads need an hour or two to rise in addition to the hands-on prep time and baking time. In this cookbook, that additional time will be included in the prep time.

Ingredients. Carefully check the ingredients. Do you have everything you need? Do you have enough of everything? Double-check any use-by dates (old yeast won't allow your bread to rise the way it should, for instance, so you might need to buy more if yours is expired). Make a shopping list. If the recipe calls for butter, eggs, or other ingredients to be "at room temperature," take them out of the refrigerator 30 minutes before you plan to begin cooking. Make sure chilled ingredients are in the refrigerator or freezer.

Equipment. Does the recipe call for a food processor or electric mixer? What size pan(s) will you need? These requirements are often buried within the instruction steps for the recipe. Once again, you don't want to get halfway through your recipe only to realize that you don't have the right size pan! The recipes in this cookbook each provide a list of required equipment to help you as you learn, but most cookbooks do not do this.

Prepare Your Work Station

» **Clear the counter.** Find enough space for working. Make sure the surface is clean, wiping it down with a sponge and kitchen cleaner before you begin.

» **Wash your hands.** Start every cooking or baking session with a thorough hand scrub using warm, soapy water. Wash your hands again any time you handle raw meat or eggs, which may carry germs.

» **Mise en place.** Gather your tools, ingredients, and recipe instructions.

Now you're finally ready to start baking!

Clean Up—Before and After

Cleanliness is a top priority in the kitchen. It prevents the spread of foodborne illnesses, reduces the risk of food contamination or cross-contamination, prevents accidents, and makes both cooking and eating what you've cooked more enjoyable.

WASH YOUR HANDS

I can't say this often enough. Always wash thoroughly using warm, soapy water.

WASH YOUR INGREDIENTS

All fruits and vegetables should be thoroughly rinsed and scrubbed as needed before using. Don't forget to wash the peel of citrus fruits (oranges, lemons, limes, etc.) if the peel or the grated zest will be used in the recipe. Meat (not ground meat), poultry, and fish should be rinsed in cold water and patted dry with paper towels.

POST-BAKING CLEANUP

Believe me, I hate cleaning as much as anyone, but if you're going to cook, *ya gotta do it*. For me, tidying up as I go (wiping up spills immediately, putting used dishes straight into the dishwasher, putting leftover ingredients away after use, etc.) makes cooking more pleasant and, most importantly, keeps me from having to face a daunting mess after I'm done with my baking project. While I do the final cleanup, I like to listen to music or a podcast, or use the time to catch up with a friend by phone.

OUCH!

Safety in the kitchen is super important. Between high temperatures and sharp tools, this room holds a number of potential hazards. Follow these guidelines to stay safe.

General Kitchen Safety

» Keep long hair tied back, long sleeves rolled up, and other loose clothing tucked away. Remove jewelry and other items that could catch on things.

» Clean up spills promptly to avoid potentially staining any surfaces, spreading bacteria, or letting pets consume anything that may be dangerous for them, like chocolate.

Cooking with Heat Safely

» If you're cooking on the stove top, stay close by, ideally in the kitchen. When baking, it's fine to be elsewhere in the house, but be sure to set a timer and keep it with you in case you lose track of time.

» Know where the fire extinguisher is kept and how to use it. You can also use baking soda to put out a small fire, so know where that is stored, too.

» Familiarize yourself with the oven and stove-top controls before you begin.

» Before turning on a burner (or burners), make sure that the stove top is clear: that there are no bits of food, spills, oven mitts, dish towels, or other flammable items on top.

» Never leave a burner turned on without a filled pan or pot on it.

» Never leave an empty pan on top of a burner that is turned on.

» Don't leave pan or pot handles sticking out where they can be bumped easily. This is especially important if there are small children in the house.

» Lighting a gas stove: A gas stove has a "pilot light," a tiny flame that burns continuously inside the stove. To turn on a burner, turn the control to the "light" (or "lite") function. This will release a small stream of gas and make a clicking sound until the gas ignites. If the flame doesn't ignite within 10 seconds or so, turn the burner back to the off position to avoid a buildup of flammable gas, and then try again. Adjust the flame to your desired level. If you are unfamiliar with your gas stove, get a parent to show you how to use it properly.

» When turning off the stove, be sure that the burner is completely off. On gas stoves, it is possible to extinguish the flame while gas is still being released. Without the flame burning, the gas will be released into the room, which creates a fire hazard and poses a risk to anyone breathing it in.

» Never put glass or ceramic pots or pans directly on a hot burner.

» Be cautious when placing hot pans, baking dishes, or pots on any surface—some surfaces are not heat resistant and can be severely damaged by a hot pot. Hot pans can rest on a wire rack if necessary until they are cool enough to avoid damaging countertops.

» Not all pans are made to go inside a hot oven. In general, most metal and glass pans are oven safe. Pans made of cast iron, enameled cast iron (like Le Creuset), copper, or uncoated stainless steel are safe for use up to 500°F. Uncoated anodized aluminum and glass dishes can be used in temperatures up to 450°F. Pans with nonstick coatings (like Teflon) and any pan with plastic handles or knobs should not be used in the oven.

» Use dry oven mitts when handling pans, pots, or pan/pot handles. Damp or wet oven mitts will actually conduct heat and may burn your hands if you use them to take a pan out of the oven. Also make sure your oven mitts are in good shape, as you can be burned in any places where they are worn thin.

» Stand back and keep small children away when opening a hot oven.

Using Sharp Knives and Other Tools

» Keep blades sharp. It may sound contradictory, but dull knives can be more dangerous than sharp ones, which are more precise and less likely to slip while cutting. Use a home knife sharpener (follow the manufacturer's instructions) or ask a parent to have your knives professionally sharpened about once a year.

» Always use a cutting board. Place food to be cut on a firm cutting board (if necessary, place a rubber mat or a slightly damp dish towel underneath the cutting board to prevent slipping). Do not cut food while you hold it in your hands.

» Use "the claw" grip to hold the food being cut. Curl your fingers under at the second knuckle like a claw and tuck your thumb behind them to protect them from the knife blade. Press firmly against the food being cut with your knuckles. This keeps your fingers away from the knife blade and is a very effective way to prevent cuts. Professional chefs are trained to use knives this way.

» Carry knives/blades carefully. Always be mindful when walking through the kitchen with a sharp object. Hold it by the handle, with the sharp tip pointed down at your side and away from yourself and others. When handing a sharp object to another person, always offer the handle first, keeping the blade pointed down and never gripping the blade.

» Keep knives clean and store them properly. Make sure handles are free of grease or slippery liquids. Store knives in a knife holder or knife drawer when not in use, and never leave knives in a sink or dish drainer where someone might reach a hand in and accidentally grab them by the sharp end.

KEY TERMINOLOGY

Baking, like any other specialty, has a language of its own. Here is a list of the baking terms you'll see in this book, along with their definitions. See the pages referenced for more details where appropriate.

» **Beat:** Stir two or more ingredients together using a handheld electric mixer, a stand mixer, or a spoon (see page 26).

» **Blind bake:** Prebake or partially bake a pie crust before adding a filling (see page 32).

» **Cream together:** Beat air into butter or another fat. Butter and sugar are often creamed together (see page 26).

» **Cut in:** Use a pastry cutter, knife, or food processor to cut butter or shortening into a bowl of flour until distributed in the flour (see page 27).

» **Divided:** Used in the ingredient list to indicate that the ingredient is added to the recipe at two or more different times, thus the quantity is "divided." For example, if a recipe calls for "1 cup of oil, divided" in the ingredient list, the instructions might tell you to use ½ cup in step 1 and the remaining ½ cup later in the recipe.

» **Dollop:** Drop by heaping spoonfuls.

» **Fold in:** Mix gently with a rubber spatula to combine one ingredient into another without deflating or releasing any air (see page 28).

» **Grease:** Coat a baking pan with butter, shortening, cooking spray, or oil (see page 29).

» **Knead:** Work dough, with either your hands or an electric mixer, to develop the gluten in the flour.

» **Let rise:** Give yeasted bread dough time for the yeast to consume the sugar, ferment it, and release the gas that will make the bread become airy.

» **Mix:** Combine two or more ingredients by stirring, whisking, or beating.

» **Sift:** Shake flour or other powdered ingredients through a sieve to remove lumps.

» **Stir:** Use a spoon or rubber spatula to mix two or more ingredients.

» **Whip:** Whisk a liquid (such as cream or egg whites) rapidly in order to fill it with air (see page 28).

» **Whisk:** Beat air into liquid or dry ingredients like eggs or flour.

EQUIPMENT

Step into the baking section of a cookware store, and you might become over-whelmed with all the different pans, mixers, and other gadgets. The good news is that for most baking projects, you only need a few basic pieces of equipment, and most of these are inexpensive. This list is meant to be a reference for you when you see equipment terms that you aren't familiar with in the recipes. You don't need to load up on all of these items before you can get started.

Take this list into the kitchen and do a quick inventory of what you already have. You'll likely find many of these pieces already hidden in the cabinets. Then, if you don't have the right equipment to make a certain recipe that you really want to try out, you can add that piece to your collection—why not add it to your birthday or holiday wish list?

» **Baking dish:** This is an oven-safe dish, usually made of glass or ceramic, that has 2-inch or higher sides. They come in various sizes including 8- or 9-inch squares, 7-by-11 inches, or 9-by-13 inches. For the recipes in this book you'll need an 8-inch square, a 9-inch square, and a 9-by-13 inch.

» **Baking sheet (aka cookie sheet):** A flat metal sheet pan with a lip on one or both short sides for gripping. A rimmed baking sheet has a short rim all the way around the edges. Both types are usually made of aluminum or steel.

» **Cake pan:** A round, square, or rectangular metal baking pan with 2-inch sides.

» **Colander:** Also known as a strainer, this is a bowl-shaped device with many holes in it. Colanders are used to drain foods like pasta, rice, or canned beans.

» **Cookie cutter:** A sharp-edged device, usually made of metal but sometimes plastic, designed to cut dough into shapes (a round cookie cutter is often used to cut biscuits).

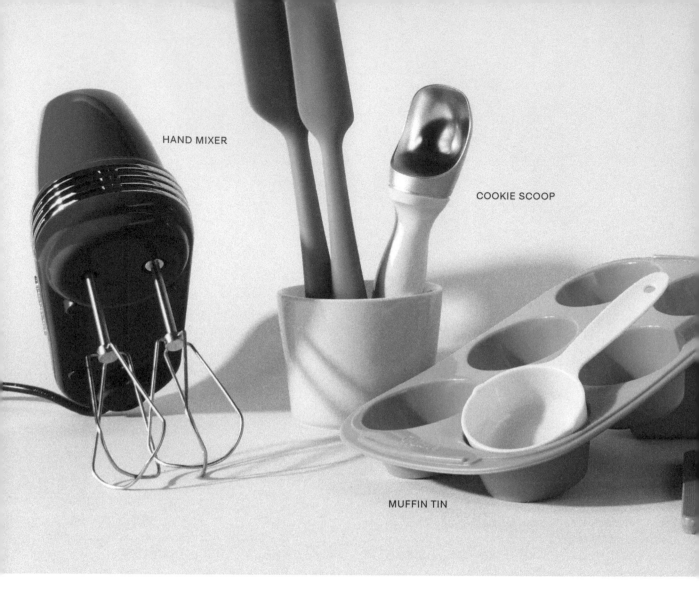

HAND MIXER

COOKIE SCOOP

MUFFIN TIN

» **Cookie scoop:** Cookie scoops are shaped like ice cream scoops and come in sizes small (1 tablespoon), medium (1½ to 2 tablespoons), and large (3 tablespoons). They are useful for portioning out cookie dough, giving you the ability to maintain consistent size and shape.

» **Cutting board:** A sturdy board, usually made of wood or durable plastic, that is used as a surface for cutting food.

FOOD PROCESSOR

CUTTING BOARD

» **Double boiler:** A set of 2 saucepots—one slightly larger than the other—that stack together with space in between. The larger one is partially filled with water and heated. The smaller one fits on top and is gently heated by the steam from the hot water in the larger pot. Double boilers are useful for melting chocolate and cooking delicate mixtures like egg custards that would quickly burn over direct heat. You can create a makeshift double boiler by putting a metal bowl over a saucepan with water in it. Don't let the bottom of the upper pot or the bowl touch the water below.

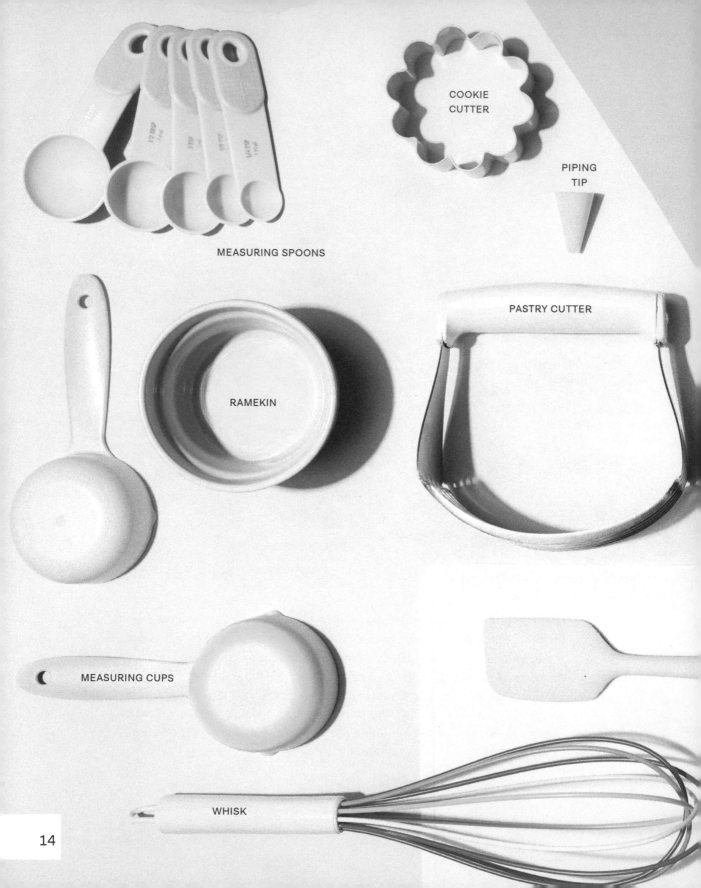

MEASURING SPOONS

COOKIE CUTTER

PIPING TIP

PASTRY CUTTER

RAMEKIN

MEASURING CUPS

WHISK

14

RUBBER SPATULA

MIXING BOWLS

ROLLING PIN

SILICONE MAT

MUFFIN LINER

» **Electric mixer:** This can be either a handheld electric mixer with two beaters attached or a stand mixer, which is a self-contained electric mixer that stands on the countertop. It has a housing that locks the beater or beaters in place over a mounting base that holds a mixing bowl.

» **Food processor:** An electric appliance that mixes and chops ingredients using interchangeable blades.

» **Loaf pan:** A baking pan, usually made of metal but sometimes made of glass or ceramic, that is shaped like a standard loaf of bread you would find at the grocery store. The standard size loaf pan is 9-by-5-by-3 inches, and that's the only size you'll need for the recipes in this book. However, 8-by-4-by-3-inch loaf pans are also common.

» **Measuring cups and spoons:** You'll need a set of dry measuring cups designed to be filled to the rim with dry ingredients and leveled off (¼, ⅓, ½, and 1 cup), a liquid measuring cup with a spout and increment markings on the side (ideally 2-cup size), and a standard set of measuring spoons (⅛ teaspoon, ¼ teaspoon, ½ teaspoon, 1 teaspoon, and 1 tablespoon).

» **Metal spatula:** A cooking utensil with a long handle and a broad, flat blade that is used primarily for lifting foods out of a skillet or pan.

» **Mixing bowls:** A set of 3 mixing bowls (small, medium, and large) for mixing ingredients. I recommend glass or ceramic mixing bowls because, unlike metal, they are "unreactive," meaning they won't react with highly acidic ingredients. The most common acidic ingredients in baking are applesauce, baking powder, brown sugar, buttermilk, chocolate, cream of tartar, non-Dutch-process cocoa powder, lemon juice, lime juice, vinegar, molasses, sour cream, and yogurt.

» **Muffin tin:** A metal pan designed specifically for baking muffins or cupcakes. A standard muffin tin has 12 wells or cups that each hold 3½ to 4 ounces of batter. A mini muffin tin usually has 24 wells or cups that each hold 1½ to 2 ounces of batter. Some recipes in this book make 18 muffins or cupcakes, so you'll need two 12-cup muffin tins to accommodate the batter. It's fine to bake with a few of the cups empty.

» **Muffin liner:** A ridged cup made of paper or silicone that is used to line a muffin tin (paper) or in place of a muffin tin (silicone) when baking cupcakes or muffins.

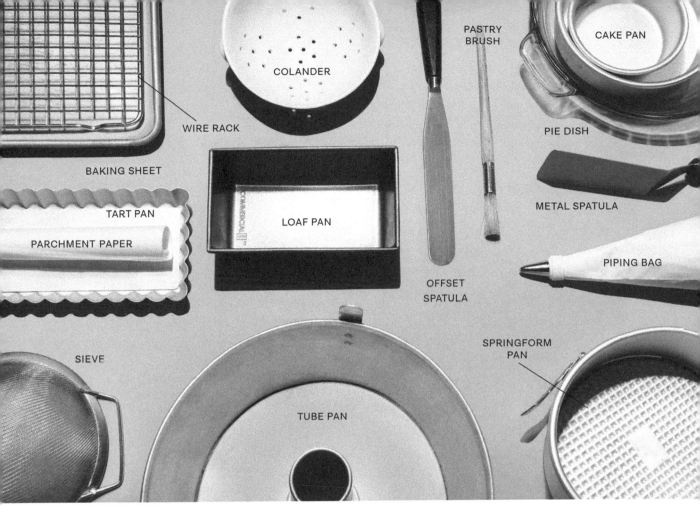

COLANDER

PASTRY BRUSH

CAKE PAN

WIRE RACK

PIE DISH

BAKING SHEET

LOAF PAN

METAL SPATULA

TART PAN

PARCHMENT PAPER

OFFSET SPATULA

PIPING BAG

SIEVE

SPRINGFORM PAN

TUBE PAN

»   **Offset spatula:** A long, narrow tool used for spreading frosting on a cake or smoothing batter into an even layer in a cake pan. An offset spatula has a handle on one end and a flat, blunt, thin metal blade at the other end.

»   **Parchment paper:** Similar to wax paper but coated with heat-resistant silicone instead of wax so it can be used in the oven. Like wax paper, parchment is both grease-resistant and moisture-resistant. You can find it in the supermarket next to the waxed paper and aluminum foil.

»   **Pastry brush:** Also called a basting brush, this brush is designed specifically for spreading glaze over pastries, cakes, and breads or applying an egg wash over a crust.

» **Pastry cutter (or pastry blender):** A tool used to mix fat (such as butter or shortening) into flour when making pastries. Pastry cutters are usually made of narrow strips of metal or wire that are attached to a handle. To use it, place the fat and flour in a mixing bowl and press the metal strips or wire into the fat to cut it into small pieces while blending it with the flour.

» **Pie plate or pie dish:** A round glass, ceramic, or metal baking dish with angled sides, designed specifically for baking pies.

» **Pie weights:** Small metal, glass, or ceramic balls used to weigh down a pie crust for blind baking (see page 32).

» **Piping (or pastry) bag:** A cone-shaped bag made of paper, cloth, or plastic that, when fitted with a piping tip, is used to squeeze batter or frosting by pressing it through a narrow opening. This is used for forming certain pastries and for decorating cakes or cookies with frosting. Don't have a piping bag? You can also use a sturdy, resealable plastic bag.

» **Piping tips:** Small metal or plastic cones with variously shaped openings. They are fitted into the open end of a piping bag and used to squeeze frosting or batter out into decorative shapes.

» **Ramekin:** An oven-safe glass or ceramic dish, usually round with straight sides, intended for both baking and serving. Ramekins come in a wide range of sizes, but the most commonly used are 4-, 6-, or 8-ounce. The recipes in this book that use ramekins call for 8-ounce ramekins.

» **Rolling pin:** Usually made of wood, a typical American-style rolling pin has a center rod controlled by two handles on the ends and turns inside an outer cylinder. A rolling pin is essential for rolling out dough to an even thickness.

» **Rubber spatula:** A flexible, rectangular rubber (or silicone) head on a long handle used for stirring, folding, spreading ingredients, and scraping mixing bowls.

» **Saucepan:** A small round cooking pot with tall sides. Usually made of metal, it is used on the stove top.

» **Sieve:** Also known as a strainer, this is a utensil used for straining solids from liquids. It consists of a handle or handles attached to a mesh (plastic or metal) bowl.

» **Silicone mat:** A reusable flat sheet of silicone that is used to line a baking pan, creating a nonstick surface.

» **Skillet (frying pan):** A round metal pan with slanted sides and a straight handle that is used on the stove top for frying, stir-frying, or sautéing.

» **Springform pan:** A round metal baking pan with removable sides often used for making cheesecakes.

» **Tart pan:** A pan with sides that are shorter than those of a pie pan (usually ¾ inch to 2 inches deep) and are often fluted (or scalloped). Tart pans are usually metal, and they come in many different shapes and sizes. The tart recipes in this book call for a round tart pan that is 9 inches across and has a removable bottom. This makes it possible to lift the whole tart out of the pan while maintaining the shape and decorative edge of your tart.

» **Tube pan (or angel food cake pan):** A round, high-sided metal baking pan with a cone-shaped hollow center, used for baking ring-shaped cakes.

» **Whisk:** A long handle with several metal or wire loops joined to it. A whisk is used to blend ingredients while incorporating air into the mixture (see page 28).

» **Wire rack:** Also known as a cooling rack, this is a platform made up of metal rods or wires set in a crisscross pattern. The rack allows air to circulate under and around hot food so it cools quickly. Some wire racks have 2 or 3 layers so you can cool a lot of cookies or other baked goods at once. You will use a wire rack at some point for cooling almost every recipe in the book, so they will not be listed as required equipment for each recipe.

THE SEVEN HABITS OF
HIGHLY SUCCESSFUL BAKERS

Baking is a fun and satisfying hobby, especially once you get comfortable with the basic techniques. Keep these best practices in mind and you'll be well on your way to becoming a master baker.

1. **Measure precisely.** In many types of cooking it's okay to improvise, but baking is an exact science. When you're baking—especially delicate cakes, pastries, and breads—if your measurements are off, your final result will be, too. Precise measuring is important for success. (See page 24 for tips on measuring.)

2. **Use the best ingredients.** This doesn't mean you have to spend a ton of money; just choose the best quality you can. The fresher your ingredients are—whether we're talking about baking soda, flour, or fruits and vegetables— the better your food will taste and look. If your bag of flour is more than a few months old, you might want to replace it. Frozen fruit is fine, but you'll get the best results using fresh. Using real vanilla extract, real maple syrup, and good-quality chocolate will elevate your baking from OK to OMG!

3. **Don't get hung up on looks.** Even if your creations aren't Instagram-worthy, they will most likely still taste delicious. Getting picture-perfect results takes a lot of practice, so keep at it and soon you'll have photogenic cakes, pies, and more.

4. **Give yourself extra time.** Things always take longer than you anticipate, and rushing through a recipe is, well, a recipe for disappointment.

5. **Don't crumble under pressure.** Before you bake a dish for an important event, try it out a few times to make sure it comes out the way you want. That way, your dish will shine when it matters.

6. **Follow directions.** The first time you make a dish, follow the recipe down to the letter. Once you know how it is supposed to turn out, go ahead and experiment to add your own spin on the dish (but of course, don't forget about rule number 1).

7. **Have fun.** Lick the bowl, make a funny-shaped cookie, give yourself a batter mustache (just don't eat dough or batter that has raw eggs in it since that can lead to food poisoning!).

2

BAKING
TECHNIQUES
and SKILLS

Baking is part science, part skill, and all fun! This chapter covers the techniques you need to know so you can confidently start baking sweet and savory creations with all your favorite flavors, textures, and ingredients.

MEASURING

By now you know that in cooking, you can often wing it with ingredients, throwing in a splash of this or a pinch of that as the urge strikes, but baking is an exact science. If you don't have the right combinations and proportions of ingredients, your cake or cookies could end up being a total flop. It is essential to use proper measuring techniques in baking.

Measuring Dry Ingredients

Measuring by weight (ounces and pounds) is the most precise way to measure dry ingredients, but since most recipes (in the United States) use volume measurements (cups, teaspoons, and tablespoons), follow these tips for the most accuracy:

» Measure larger quantities of dry ingredients in scoop-shaped measuring cups (usually made of plastic or metal). Fill the cup so that the ingredient is mounded over the top edge, and then level off the top with the flat side of a knife.

» When measuring very light ingredients like flour or cornstarch, use the "spoon-and-level" method to avoid packing the ingredient too tightly into the measuring cup (giving you more of the ingredient than required): Spoon the ingredient from the container into the measuring cup until it is mounded up over the brim, and then level it off with the flat side of a knife.

» Scoop up larger grainy ingredients like sugar using the measuring cup and then level off the top using the flat edge of a knife or just by shaking the excess off. Brown sugar is always (unless otherwise noted) measured "packed," which means it is pressed into the measuring cup so that it is firm and there is little space between the grains.

» Use measuring spoons to measure dry ingredients in quantities smaller than ¼ cup.

Measuring Wet / Liquid Ingredients

» When measuring liquid in ¼-cup or larger quantities, use transparent measuring cups (usually made of glass) placed flat on the counter. Pour the liquid into the measuring cup slowly. Get down to eye level with the cup and stop pouring when the level of liquid is at the desired measurement line.

>> Use measuring spoons to measure liquids in teaspoon or tablespoon quantities. Fill the spoon so that the liquid comes up to the top edge and is flat across the top.

MELTING

There is more to melting than you might think. Ingredients like butter are fairly simple, but it's important to follow the instructions for melting chocolate to avoid burning it.

Melting Butter

Butter can be melted in a small saucepan on the stove top over medium heat, or in the microwave, covered, in a small, microwave-safe dish, in 30- to 60-second intervals. Note that "at room temperature" butter should not be melted but instead should be set on the counter until it is room temperature, which will take about 30 minutes if the butter has been refrigerated and about 60 minutes if the butter has been frozen. Other cookbooks may refer to room temperature butter as "softened."

Melting Chocolate

Chocolate must be melted slowly, using gentle heat, or it will burn or become grainy. If you try to melt chocolate in a saucepan over a burner, it won't turn out well. Instead, use one of the following methods to achieve perfectly melted chocolate.

Melting chocolate in a microwave: This is usually the quickest way to melt chocolate. Chop the chocolate into small, fairly equal-size pieces and place in a microwave-safe bowl. Set the microwave's power to 50 percent or the low setting, then microwave for 30 to 60 seconds. Remove the bowl from the microwave and stir until the chocolate is completely melted and smooth. If the chocolate is not completely melted after stirring, microwave for another 30 seconds. Repeat microwaving in 30-second intervals, stirring in between, until the chocolate is completely melted and smooth.

Melting chocolate in a double boiler: Before there were microwaves, a double boiler made it possible to melt chocolate without burning it. A true double boiler is a pair of saucepans that stack (one on top of the other) with simmering water in the lower one and the chocolate that will be melted in the top. (Double boilers are also useful for cooking delicate mixtures like custards and pastry cream.) You can fashion your own double boiler by putting water in a saucepan and then placing a heat-safe bowl (ideally metal) on top to hold the chocolate. In either case, fill the bottom pan with about 1 inch of water and bring to a simmer (the water should be moving, with lots of tiny bubbles, but not actively boiling). Once the water is simmering, reduce the heat to low. Place the chocolate in the top pan or bowl and set it over the simmering water. Make sure that the bowl or the top pan is not actually touching the water (or else the chocolate could burn). Stir the chocolate continuously until it is completely melted and smooth, then remove from the heat.

Melting chocolate in liquid: Chocolate can be safely melted in a liquid (such as cream). Combine the liquid and chocolate (cut into small pieces) in a saucepan over moderate heat. Use about 1 tablespoon of liquid per ounce of chocolate. Heat, stirring, until the chocolate is completely melted and the mixture is smooth.

MIXING

You might not think that the act of mixing would require its own section, but there are actually a surprising number of ways to combine ingredients together, and sometimes your results are largely dependent on choosing the right one. Here are the most common mixing terms you'll see:

Beating: Stirring ingredients together using a handheld electric mixer, a stand mixer, or a spoon.

Creaming: You'll notice that many baking recipes begin with "cream together the butter and sugar" or a similar instruction. This is a way of mixing the butter and sugar together to create a light, fluffy structure for cakes and other baked goods. The process of creaming is used to combine fat (like butter or shortening) with sugar by beating them together. But creaming isn't as much about mixing the two ingredients together as it is about *aerating* the fat, or filling it with air. By folding the butter (or fat) over and over in the beating process, you create tiny air bubbles in it. Grains of sugar cut into the fat and magnify this effect.

To properly cream together butter or other fats such as vegetable shortening with sugar, start with room-temperature (or slightly cooler, but not any warmer!) butter. Measure the butter and sugar into a large mixing bowl and, using a handheld electric mixer or a stand mixer, beat on medium speed until the mixture is light and fluffy. This will take about 5 minutes. If you watch carefully, you'll notice that the color of the mixture will become visibly paler, which is one way to tell when it's done. You can cream butter by hand using a fork or a wooden spoon, but it will take significantly longer—and your beating arm will get a workout!

Cutting in: Cutting in means combining fat (such as butter or shortening) with flour. The purpose of cutting in is to distribute pea-size bits of fat throughout the dough. This technique is used in making pastries like pie crusts, scones, and biscuits. In the high heat of the oven, the fat melts, creating steam, which makes air pockets in the dough. It's the secret to flaky pastry crust!

You can cut in using a food processor, pastry cutter, the back of a fork, or two knives. Whichever method you choose, always start with fat that is very cold and cut into small pieces.

» **To use a food processor:** Fit the processor with the steel S blade. Put the flour in the bowl of the processor, and add the butter or other fat. Pulse the processor repeatedly until the mixture is in pea-size crumbs or a coarse meal.

» **To do it by hand:** Place the flour in a mixing bowl, and toss the cold butter pieces on top. Use a pastry cutter, fork, or two knives to smash and/or slice the butter into smaller and smaller bits until you have a mixture of flour and butter in pea-size clumps.

Folding: This is a gentle type of mixing that includes an airy, whipped ingredient (such as whipped cream or egg whites) that you don't want to deflate. Add the lighter ingredient (whipped cream, for example) to the heavier ingredient (like berries), then use a rubber spatula to gently fold the mixture on top of itself, turning the bowl after each fold, until the ingredients are combined.

Stirring: Stirring is just plain old hand mixing with a spoon, whisk, or rubber spatula. Dry ingredients and thin liquid mixtures can be stirred together.

Whipping or whisking: When you want to add lots of air into an ingredient to make it light and fluffy, as with whipped cream or egg whites for meringue, you whip it. It's easiest to whip using an electric hand mixer or stand mixer set on medium-high speed, but you can do it by hand with a whisk if you've got the stamina.

HOW TO MAKE WHIPPED CREAM

To make your own whipped cream, put 1 cup of heavy whipping cream in a large mixing bowl. Add 2 tablespoons of granulated sugar. Using a wire whisk or an electric mixer, whip the cream until it holds soft peaks. This will take about 5 minutes with an electric mixer and about twice that long if whipping by hand. The flavor of homemade whipped cream is well worth the effort, though there are quality canned whipped creams sold at the grocery store. Look for those made with real cream for the best flavor.

PREPARING PANS

When a recipe calls for greasing the pan, it means coating the inside of a baking pan with a thin layer of fat (oil, shortening, or butter) before adding the batter or dough. This prevents food from sticking to the pan during baking.

To grease a pan: Use nonstick cooking spray, or use a paper towel to spread a tablespoon or two of room-temperature butter, oil, or shortening all over the inside of the pan. Whichever method you choose, make sure to get the fat into the corners, up the sides, and over the entire bottom of the inside of the pan.

To grease and flour a pan: Sometimes a recipe will call for both greasing and flouring a pan. Grease as instructed above, then sprinkle a small handful of flour over the pan. Lightly tilt and shake the pan around so that the flour evenly coats the entire inside of the pan (don't forget the corners), then tip any excess flour out into the sink.

HANDLING EGGS

Eggs are a crucial part of many baking recipes. They bind ingredients together and help them rise, too. When you buy eggs, be sure to check the size. Most recipes assume that you are using large eggs, so unless otherwise noted, choose that size. Eggs also come in medium, extra-large, and jumbo, so read the carton ahead of time.

Cracking Eggs

I love cracking eggs. There is just something about the crunching of a delicate egg shell splitting apart that I find incredibly satisfying. The most common method is to whack it—firmly, but not too firmly—against the edge of a bowl or on a flat, hard surface like a countertop. Pry the shell open at the crack and pour the egg out. If you are adding eggs to other ingredients, crack them into a separate bowl first so you don't risk getting egg shell in the other ingredients.

So, what do you do when you get a bit of egg shell in your bowl? Use wet fingers, a spoon, or—my favorite—a larger piece of egg shell to corral the piece of shell over to the side of the bowl and scoop it out. The egg shell method works the best because it has a sharp edge that can cut through the egg white, allowing you to isolate the bit of shell quicker than you can with your fingers or a spoon.

Separating Eggs

When a recipe requires just egg yolks or just egg whites, or simply for the whites and yolks to be added at different times, you need to separate the two. Always start with cold eggs right out of the refrigerator, as these are easier to separate than warmer eggs. Crack the egg as you normally would, but when you open up the shell, let the white part fall out into the bowl below while you hold the yolk in one side of the shell. Then move the egg yolk back and forth between the two shell halves, letting any excess white fall into the bowl. Place the yolk in a separate bowl.

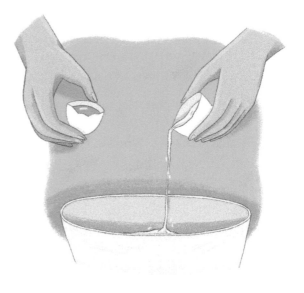

When you want fluffy egg whites (for meringue, soufflé, etc.), it's important to keep egg yolk out of the whites. If you are separating several eggs, use a small bowl to collect each white, then transfer it to a larger bowl so you are collecting one egg white at a time. That way, if you get a little yolk in the white, you can throw that one away, clean the small bowl, and start again. The rest of the whites you just separated will be safe and untainted in the big bowl.

Whipping Egg Whites

Some dishes, like soufflés, mousses, and meringues, are meant to be fluffy, light, and full of air. To accomplish this, egg whites must be *aerated*, or whipped full of air. Start with room-temperature egg whites. If the eggs are straight out of the refrigerator, warm the whites up a bit by placing the bowl of egg whites in a larger bowl that has a few inches of lukewarm water in it. Let one bowl sit in the other for a few minutes, taking care not to splash any water into the eggs.

Use a whisk or an electric handheld or stand mixer fitted with a whisk attachment to whip your egg whites. An electric mixer is obviously quicker and easier. Whichever utensil you choose, make sure it is clean and dry before you begin.

Put the egg whites in a large, clean, and completely dry glass, ceramic, or metal bowl. Beat at low speed until the whites become foamy. Raise the speed to medium or medium-high and continue to beat. If you beat the whites too long, they will actually start to deflate. That's why it's good to add a pinch of cream of tartar at this stage. The tartar will help stabilize the whites so they keep their airy shape.

Soft peaks: If the recipe calls for egg whites to be beaten to "soft peaks," beat until the whites form mounds that flop over a little when you pull out the whisk or beater.

Stiff peaks: If the recipe calls for "stiff peaks," keep beating for a few more minutes until the whites are smooth, glossy, and form a peak that holds its shape when you pull out the whisk or beater.

Tempering Eggs

When a recipe calls for adding eggs to a hot liquid, you need to "temper" the eggs. Tempering raises the temperature of eggs enough so when you add them to a hot liquid, the eggs won't start cooking from the heat of the liquid.

To temper eggs: Add a small amount (¼ to ½ cup) of the warm liquid to the eggs and whisk continuously. Once the small amount of liquid has been thoroughly whisked into the eggs, you can add that mixture back into the remaining warm liquid.

PASTRY DOUGH

Making a good pie or pastry crust is easier than it looks. There are a few important rules to follow for good results, but with a bit of practice, you'll make perfect pies, tarts, and pastries with crusts that are light, flaky, beautifully golden brown, and that hold their shape when baked.

Making Pastry Dough

» Make sure your butter (or other fat) is very cold. Refrigerate it for several hours before you plan to make your pastry or, better yet, leave it in the freezer overnight.

» Follow the instructions for cutting butter into flour (see page 27). Add other ingredients at this time, too, like sugar or salt, according to whatever recipe you are following.

>> Add ice water a little at a time and mix until the crumbly flour-and-butter mixture comes together in a ball.

>> Flatten the ball into a disk shape, and wrap it tightly in plastic wrap. Refrigerate it for at least 30 minutes. This will chill the fat in the dough enough to make it easy to handle.

Rolling Out Dough

When you are ready to roll out your pastry dough, remove it from the refrigerator, unwrap it, and place it on a lightly floured work surface (a surface you have sprinkled with a thin layer of flour). Lightly dust the top of the disk of dough with flour. Using a heavy rolling pin, roll from the center of the dough away from your body. Lift the dough and turn it 90 degrees, then roll again from the center away from your body. Continue turning and rolling in this manner until the dough is the thickness and size required for the recipe. Check to make sure that the thickness of your dough is even throughout. For most of the recipes in this book, a thickness of about ⅛ inch is ideal. To transfer a large piece of dough to a pie plate or tart pan, roll it onto the rolling pin and then unroll it from the rolling pin onto the baking pan.

Crimping Dough

Crimping dough is folding or pinching the edges of pastry to create a finished, decorative rim. To crimp a pie crust, press the index finger of one hand against the edge of the dough from inside the pie tin. Then, with the thumb and index finger of the other hand pressed together to make a V, push the dough around the tip of the other index finger from the outside. Do this all the way around the pie plate to give the pie a scalloped edge.

Blind Baking Pastry Crust

Blind baking is pre-baking or partially baking the crust of a pie or tart before adding the filling. The moisture in many pie fillings can prevent the crust from cooking through and leave you with a soggy bottom. We don't want that! Partially baking the crust (about halfway) will keep the crust firm and prevent the filling from soaking in. Blind baking is also used for pies with fillings that aren't baked (like a banana cream pie), so you add the filling to a fully baked crust.

A blind-baked crust can puff up and the sides can droop during baking. To avoid that, fill the pan with weights to help the crust keep its shape during baking.

To blind bake a crust: After placing the dough in the baking pan, line it with parchment paper or aluminum foil. Add something heavy like pie weights (see page 18), dried beans, rice, or something similar that you find around your kitchen that is relatively heavy (but not too heavy!), heat-safe, and food-safe. Bake until the edges of the crust turn golden brown. For a half-baked crust, this should take 10 to 15 minutes. For a fully baked crust, bake with the weights for 10 minutes, remove the weights, and continue to bake until the bottom is golden brown, 8 to 10 minutes more.

To dock pie dough: If you don't have pie weights or something else suitable, you can "dock" the crust by poking holes all over the bottom of the unbaked crust with the tines of a fork. This also helps prevent the crust from puffing up as it bakes, though it is not as effective as weights.

YEASTED DOUGH

Yeast is used in doughs that need to rise, like bread. As the dough sits in a warm place, the yeast consumes the sugars in the dough, ferments them, and releases gases (carbon dioxide and alcohol) that cause the dough to increase in size.

Proofing Yeast

Many yeasted bread recipes begin with a proofing step. This step ensures that your yeast is alive and healthy before you do all the mixing and kneading of the dough.

To proof yeast: Combine the yeast and a pinch of sugar with lukewarm water according to your recipe instructions. Let the mixture stand for 5 to 10 minutes or until the mixture becomes foamy. The foaminess is the "proof" that your yeast is good to go. Continue with the recipe, adding the flour and other ingredients. (Sometimes you will see recipes that refer to proofing *dough*, which generally means letting the final, shaped dough rise a second [or final] time before baking. Don't confuse the two.)

Kneading Dough

Kneading dough is the process of working the dough with your hands (or a stand mixer) to help the protein gluten develop. Gluten is the backbone of bread, giving it structure and strength and trapping the gas released by the yeast, causing the bread to rise.

Kneading bread dough by hand takes 10 to 15 minutes. Using a stand mixer cuts the time to 5 to 8 minutes.

To knead dough by hand: Place the dough on a lightly floured work surface. Sprinkle the dough with a bit of flour and, using the heels of your hands, push the dough down and away from your body, flattening it. Fold the flattened dough back over itself, then flatten it again with the heels of your hands. After a few repetitions, turn the dough 90 degrees and continue in the same fashion. As you are kneading, add flour, a tablespoon or so at a time, as needed to keep the dough from sticking to your hands or the work surface. Continue kneading until the dough is smooth and supple. This will take 10 to 15 minutes.

To knead dough with a stand mixer: Put the dough in the bowl of a stand mixer. Fit the mixer with its dough hook and let it run for 5 to 8 minutes, at medium-low speed, until the dough is smooth and supple.

Letting Dough Rise

Once yeast dough has been proofed, mixed, and kneaded, it needs time to rise. Choose a large bowl (large enough to allow your dough to expand to at least twice its original size), and coat it lightly with about a tablespoon of oil. Place the dough in the bowl, and turn it over so it is lightly coated all over with oil. Cover the bowl with a clean dish towel and set it in a warm (but not hot), non-drafty place. This could be your kitchen counter, on top of your clothes dryer, or even inside your oven (with the oven turned off!). Let the dough rise until it has doubled in size, 60 to 90 minutes.

DECORATING CAKES AND COOKIES

There are so many fun, easy ways to decorate cakes and cookies. Gel food coloring comes in wonderfully intense colors, and just a few drops in a bowl of frosting can create some beautiful hues. Sprinkles also come in bright and pastel colors, and the shapes and textures can really add a lot of pizzazz to a cake or cookie. The best part? They are really easy to find at craft stores, cake decorating shops, and even your local grocery store.

Frosting Cakes and Cupcakes

Cakes and cupcakes are often decorated with frosting (also called icing—the terms are sometimes interchangeable, though icing is generally thinner and glossier). There are a few different ways to apply frosting to cakes or cupcakes, each allowing you to create different visual effects.

Knife or spatula: Using a knife or spatula is the simplest method for spreading frosting evenly over an entire cake.

Piping: For a fancier look and for additional decorations on your cake or cupcakes, use a piping bag (a sturdy, resealable plastic bag with one corner snipped off also works well) to apply frosting in decorative patterns on the cake. Piping bags are fitted with piping tips or nozzles in various shapes. This is how cake decorators make flowers, borders, and other designs using buttercream frosting.

» Cut off about half an inch from the tip of the piping bag and insert a piping tip (see page 18). Place the piping bag, tip down, in a tall glass or pitcher and fold the bag down over the sides. Using a rubber spatula, scoop frosting into the bag, filling it about two-thirds full. Close the bag tightly, pushing out any air pockets, and secure the end with a twist tie or a rubber band.

» To begin piping, hold the bag straight up and down, about half an inch above your cake, and squeeze the bag from the top to apply the frosting. You can create all kinds of effects using different shaped tips. Smooth, even piping takes a little practice, so don't worry if your first efforts aren't that great. Practice piping on a piece of parchment paper first to get the hang of it.

» To pipe frosting onto cupcakes, start at the outer edge and gently squeeze the bag from the top, slowly working your way around the cupcake in an outside-in spiral. When you get to the center, stop squeezing and pull the tip straight up and away from the top of the cupcake.

To frost a layer cake: I like to level off the cake layers (use a serrated knife to cut off the top of each cake layer so the surface is flat and even) and then add a "crumb coat," a thin layer of frosting intended to seal in the crumbs so they don't get mixed up in the main frosting layer. By starting with a crumb coat, you'll ensure that your cake ends up looking neat and tidy.

» Level your cake layers, and stack them with frosting in between the layers. The top cake layer should be placed upside down—so that the part that was the bottom during baking, which is smooth, is now on top.

» Coat the entire cake—top and sides—with a very thin layer of frosting using an offset spatula. As you work, wipe any crumbs off the spatula with a paper towel, and avoid getting any crumbs into the bowl of frosting. Refrigerate the cake for 15 to 30 minutes to firm up the crumb coat.

>> To add more frosting and create a nice, thick layer of frosting over the top and sides of the cake, begin by using the offset spatula to smooth the sides and top. This will make it easier to apply the final coat of frosting. Once the cake is covered with this final layer of frosting, use the tip of the knife or the spatula to create designs or patterns.

Decorating Cookies

Icing for cookies is usually a mixture of powdered sugar and milk. The more milk, the thinner the icing. Add food coloring to make different colors. A piping bag, a resealable plastic bag with the tip cut off, or a plastic squeeze bottle are all great for thinner icing and are perfect for adding decorative details to cookies.

TIPS, TRICKS, AND BAKING WISDOM

Here are my favorite baking tips, tricks, and bits of wisdom that will help you become the world's next great baker.

Check the Oven Temperature

There's no way around it: Ovens don't always heat to the precise temperature you set them to. If they under-heat, your baked goods may take longer to cook. If they overheat, your baked goods might burn if you leave them for the amount of time specified in the recipe. If you find that you are consistently having to adjust cooking times, it's a good idea to get an oven thermometer and check your oven's accuracy. You can buy a simple, inexpensive oven thermometer at any kitchen supply or hardware store, and you may even find one at the supermarket.

Follow Instructions for Using Ingredients at a Certain Temperature

If a recipe begins with creaming butter and sugar together, using room-temperature butter will give you a much better result than trying to cream a rock-hard block of butter straight from the refrigerator. For pastry crust, when you want to cut butter into flour to create pockets of air, cold butter is a must. To proof yeast, you'll need warm water or it won't proof correctly.

When combining ingredients, you generally want them to be at similar temperatures. For instance, you don't want to add cold eggs to hot melted chocolate.

Pay Attention to the Order of Steps in the Recipe

All the ingredients are eventually going to be mixed together, so why can't you just dump them all in at once and stir? Because when it comes to baking, the order of the steps matters. For instance, when a recipe calls for creaming butter and sugar together before adding the eggs and other wet ingredients, it's because you want the butter to become aerated (filled with air) so your final product will have a light and airy texture, rather than being heavy and dense.

Rotate Pans During Baking

All ovens have hot spots—areas where heat concentrates. Rotating your pans—from back to front and from top to bottom—during baking will help your treats bake evenly.

Store Baked Goods Properly

You can make many baked goods ahead of time and keep them fresh until serving. Always let baked goods cool completely to room temperature before wrapping or covering them in plastic wrap or placing them in a storage container. These storage tips will keep your baked goods fresh and delicious:

» **Unfrosted cakes, cupcakes, and muffins:** Store in an airtight container at room temperature for 3 to 5 days, or freeze in resealable plastic bags for up to 3 months (thaw in the refrigerator overnight before frosting).

» **Frosted cakes and cupcakes:** The frosting acts as a seal, so you can skip the tight plastic wrap. Instead, cover lightly (don't smoosh your frosting!) with plastic wrap or aluminum foil and store at room temperature for up to 5 days. If the cake has been cut, wrap the cut sides in plastic wrap.

» **Cookies:** Store soft cookies in an airtight container and crunchy cookies in a loosely covered container. Both types can be stored at room temperature for 3 to 5 days. Cookies can also be frozen for up to 3 months in an airtight container (lay parchment or wax paper in between layers).

>> **Brownies and bars:** Cover the pan of brownies tightly with plastic wrap or remove from the pan and wrap tightly in plastic. Store at room temperature for up to 3 days. Cut brownies can be stored in an airtight container (lay parchment or wax paper in between layers) for up to 3 days or frozen for up to 3 months.

>> **Pies and tarts:** Cover fruit pies with plastic wrap and store at room temperature for up to 2 days or in the refrigerator for 3 to 5 days. Uncut fruit pies can be frozen, tightly wrapped with plastic wrap, for up to 3 months. Uncooked fruit pies can be frozen for up to 3 months and then baked without thawing. Pies with egg-based fillings (like pumpkin), custard, and cream pies can be stored, covered with plastic wrap, in the refrigerator for up to 4 days.

Know Your Audience

Do you or any of the people you might cook for have any special dietary restrictions?

This book offers recipes that are nut-free, gluten-free, and dairy-free. Each recipe is labeled accordingly.

TIMING REALLY IS EVERYTHING

In the world of baking, timing is super important. Use a timer whenever you put something in the oven. If a range of times is given (like "Bake for 15 to 20 minutes"), set the timer for the shorter of the two times, and check it as soon as it *might* be done. When melting chocolate, cooking sugar, or making any kind of egg-based custard, watch the pot carefully—it can scorch quite quickly.

Sweet

Recipes

PART TWO

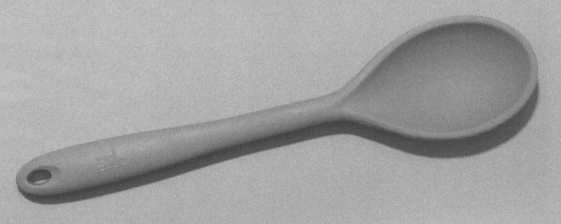

3

BREAKFAST TREATS

The recipes in this chapter are perfect for quick grab-and-go breakfasts on rushed schooldays when you want something fast. They are also terrific for lazy weekend mornings or brunches.

Note: Many of these bake up pretty quickly, like the muffins and biscuits, while others, like the croissants, require more time.

DESSERT FOR BREAKFAST!

Your mother was right: Breakfast is the most important meal of the day. But just because the morning meal is good for you doesn't mean it can't also be delicious—and sweet. The trick is to balance out any sweet ingredients with healthy ones like fresh fruits, whole grains, and low-fat dairy products.

Whole-grain muffins and banana bread are great examples of a breakfast foods that cover both the healthy and the sweet, whether they're studded with blueberries or chocolate chips. Even fruit tarts can be healthy enough to make a good breakfast.

So, the answer is yes, go ahead and eat dessert for breakfast! Just be thoughtful about which desserts actually have healthy ingredients that will keep you energized until lunch.

GLAZED LEMON SCONES

Prep time: 15 MINUTES, PLUS 15 MINUTES TO SET   *Cook time:* 25 MINUTES   *Makes:* 8 SCONES

LEVEL

NUT-FREE

EQUIPMENT

Large baking sheet, parchment paper, large mixing bowl or food processor, pastry cutter (or a fork or two knives), rolling pin, pastry brush, medium mixing bowl

2¼ cups all-purpose flour, plus more for dusting

¼ cup granulated sugar

1 tablespoon baking powder

2 tablespoons finely grated lemon zest

1 teaspoon kosher salt

½ cup (1 stick) unsalted butter, chilled and cut into small pieces

1 cup heavy (whipping) cream, plus more for brushing

1 cup confectioners' sugar

¼ cup freshly squeezed lemon juice

These simple scones deliver a surprising burst of lemony flavor in both the dough and the powdered sugar glaze. You can make these in less than an hour, so they are perfect for that school bake sale you forgot about! Scones are also a traditional part of a fancy brunch.

1. **PREHEAT THE OVEN AND PREPARE THE PAN.** Preheat the oven to 375°F. Line a large baking sheet with parchment paper.

2. **COMBINE THE DRY INGREDIENTS.** In a large mixing bowl or the bowl of a food processor, combine the flour, granulated sugar, baking powder, lemon zest, and salt.

3. **CUT IN THE BUTTER.** If using a food processor, add the butter and pulse until the mixture resembles a coarse meal. If mixing by hand, cut the butter into the dry ingredients using a pastry cutter, a fork, or two knives. Add the cup of heavy cream, and mix until combined.

4. **KNEAD, ROLL, CUT, AND BAKE.** On a lightly floured surface, knead the dough just until it holds together. Sprinkle a bit of flour on top of the dough, and use a rolling pin to roll it out into a 9-by-6-inch rectangle. Cut the dough into 8 equal-size pieces. Transfer the scones to the prepared baking sheet and brush with cream. Bake in the preheated oven for about 25 minutes, until the scones are firm and golden brown on the outside. Transfer to a wire rack to cool.

5. **MAKE THE GLAZE.** In a medium bowl, stir together the confectioners' sugar and lemon juice. Once the scones have cooled, brush the glaze over their tops.

6. **SERVE.** Let stand for about 15 minutes, until the glaze has set, and serve at room temperature.

BLUEBERRY YOGURT MUFFINS

Prep time: 10 MINUTES, PLUS 5 MINUTES TO REST   *Cook time:* 20 MINUTES   *Makes:* 12 MUFFINS

LEVEL 1

NUT-FREE

EQUIPMENT

Standard 12-cup muffin tin, 12 paper muffin liners (or oil), large mixing bowl, medium mixing bowl, rubber spatula, wooden skewer or toothpick

⅔ cup vegetable oil, plus more for greasing (if needed)

2 ½ cups all-purpose flour

1 tablespoon baking powder

1 teaspoon baking soda

½ cup granulated sugar, plus 2 tablespoons for sprinkling

2 eggs, lightly beaten

1 cup plain Greek yogurt (whole or low-fat)

¼ cup (whole or low-fat) milk

1 ½ cups fresh or frozen (thawed) blueberries

A fluffy, moist, slightly sweet blueberry muffin is a great way to start the day. These are delicious, and yet they aren't as full of sugar as the kind you get at your local bakery or coffee shop. If you want them to be sweeter and have a little crunch, you can add a sprinkle of raw or turbinado sugar over the top.

1. **PREHEAT THE OVEN AND PREPARE THE PAN.** Preheat the oven to 375°F. Line a standard 12-cup muffin tin with paper liners or grease the cups well.

2. **MIX THE DRY INGREDIENTS.** In a large mixing bowl, stir together the flour, baking powder, baking soda, and ½ cup of sugar.

3. **MIX THE WET INGREDIENTS.** In a medium mixing bowl, combine the eggs, ⅔ cup of oil, Greek yogurt, and milk.

4. **COMBINE THE WET AND DRY INGREDIENTS.** Stir the wet mixture into the dry mixture just until combined, and then fold in the blueberries using a rubber spatula.

5. **BAKE THE MUFFINS.** Scoop the batter into the prepared muffin tin, dividing evenly to fill all 12 muffin cups. Sprinkle the remaining 2 tablespoons of sugar over the tops of the muffins. Bake in the preheated oven for 18 to 20 minutes, until the tops are domed and golden brown. Test for doneness by inserting a wooden skewer or toothpick into the center of one of the muffins. If it comes out clean, the muffins are done.

6. **COOL AND SERVE.** Remove the tin from the oven and let rest for about 5 minutes before transferring the muffins to a wire rack to cool completely. Enjoy at room temperature.

OATMEAL-CHOCOLATE CHIP MUFFINS

Prep time: 10 MINUTES, PLUS 1 HOUR TO SOAK THE OATS *Cook time:* 20 MINUTES *Makes:* 12 MUFFINS

LEVEL

NUT-FREE

EQUIPMENT
Large mixing bowl, standard 12-cup muffin tin, 12 paper muffin liners (or oil), medium mixing bowl, rubber spatula, wooden skewer or toothpick

1 cup old-fashioned rolled oats (not quick cooking)

1 cup (whole or low-fat) milk

¼ cup vegetable oil, plus more for greasing (if needed)

1 cup all-purpose flour

1 teaspoon baking soda

¼ teaspoon salt

1 egg

⅓ cup brown sugar

2 teaspoons vanilla extract

1 cup semisweet chocolate chips

These muffins are the perfect excuse for eating chocolate for breakfast, and they make a nice afternoon snack, too. They combine a healthy whole grain (oats) with the sweet treat of melty chocolate chips. If you want to punch up the nutrition factor, replace the all-purpose flour with whole-wheat flour.

1. **SOAK THE OATS.** In a large mixing bowl, stir together the oats and milk. Let stand for about an hour so the oats can absorb some of the milk and become soft.

2. **PREHEAT THE OVEN AND PREPARE THE PAN.** Preheat the oven to 400°F. Line a standard 12-cup muffin tin with paper liners or grease the cups well.

3. **MIX THE DRY INGREDIENTS.** In a medium mixing bowl, stir together the flour, baking soda, and salt.

4. **COMBINE THE BATTER INGREDIENTS.** Add the egg, sugar, ¼ cup of oil, and vanilla to the oat-milk mixture and stir just until combined. Add the dry mixture to the oat mixture, and stir to combine. Using a rubber spatula, fold in the chocolate chips.

5. **BAKE THE MUFFINS.** Scoop the batter into the prepared muffin tin, dividing evenly to fill all 12 muffin cups. Bake in the preheated oven for 18 to 20 minutes, until the tops are golden brown and a wooden skewer or toothpick inserted into the center comes out clean.

6. **COOL AND SERVE.** Remove the tin from the oven, transfer the muffins to a wire rack, and let cool. Serve warm or at room temperature.

PEANUT BUTTER-FILLED BANANA MUFFINS

Prep time: 10 MINUTES, PLUS 30 MINUTES TO FREEZE THE FILLING   *Cook time:* 20 MINUTES
Makes: 12 MUFFINS

LEVEL

DAIRY-FREE

EQUIPMENT

Baking sheet or large plate, wax paper or parchment paper, standard 12-cup muffin tin, 12 paper muffin liners (or oil), medium mixing bowl, whisk, large mixing bowl, wooden skewer or toothpick

¼ cup peanut butter

½ cup vegetable oil, plus more for greasing (if needed)

1⅔ cups all-purpose flour

1 teaspoon baking soda

½ teaspoon salt

½ teaspoon ground cinnamon

¾ cup granulated sugar

2 eggs

2 very ripe bananas, mashed

1 teaspoon vanilla extract

One of my favorite quick breakfasts is peanut butter and banana on toast. These muffins take that concept to the next level—a banana bread–like muffin oozing with a molten peanut butter center. (Psst . . . go ahead and stir a few chocolate chips into the batter. I won't tell anyone!)

1. PREPARE THE FILLING. Line a baking sheet or large plate with a piece of wax paper or parchment. Spoon 12 spoonfuls of peanut butter onto the paper in separate dollops (about 1 teaspoon each). Place the sheet or plate in the freezer and freeze for 20 to 30 minutes, until the peanut butter is firm.

2. PREHEAT THE OVEN AND PREPARE THE PAN. Preheat the oven to 375°F. Line a 12-cup muffin tin with paper liners or grease well.

3. MIX THE DRY INGREDIENTS. In a medium mixing bowl, whisk together the flour, baking soda, salt, and cinnamon.

4. MAKE THE BATTER. In a large mixing bowl, whisk together the sugar, ½ cup of oil, and eggs. Mix in the mashed bananas and the vanilla. Add the dry mixture to the wet mixture, and stir just until combined.

5. FILL THE MUFFIN TIN AND BAKE THE MUFFINS. Scoop the batter into the prepared muffin tin, dividing evenly to fill all 12 muffin cups. Drop one frozen peanut butter dollop onto the center of each cup of batter, and use your finger to press it down into the center of the batter so it is completely covered. Bake in the preheated oven for 18 to 22 minutes, until a wooden skewer or toothpick inserted into muffin comes out clean. Remove the tin from the oven, transfer the muffins to a wire rack, and let cool. Serve warm or at room temperature.

BANANA NUT BREAD

Prep time: 15 MINUTES   *Cook time:* 60 MINUTES   *Makes:* 1 LOAF

LEVEL 1

EQUIPMENT

9-by-5-by-3-inch loaf pan, stand mixer or large mixing bowl with electric mixer, medium mixing bowl, wooden skewer or toothpick

½ cup unsalted butter, at room temperature, plus more for greasing

1 cup granulated sugar

2 eggs, at room temperature, lightly beaten

½ teaspoon vanilla extract

3 ripe bananas, mashed

1¼ cups all-purpose flour

1 teaspoon baking soda

½ teaspoon salt

½ cup nuts, toasted and chopped (pecans, walnuts, hazelnuts, or a combo)

Tip

Store any leftovers at room temperature, wrapped in plastic, for up to 3 days.

Quick breads (breads that use baking soda instead of yeast and don't need time to rise) are so versatile! This banana nut bread can be a special breakfast bread for your family, or you can bring it to a potluck brunch or sell it at your next bake sale. It's an easy recipe to master, and I guarantee you'll get requests to make it again and again. Walnuts are the standard in banana bread, but I like to mix it up by using hazelnuts or pecans when I have them. This is another recipe that works well with a handful of chocolate chips mixed into the batter.

1. **PREHEAT THE OVEN AND PREPARE THE PAN.** Preheat the oven to 350°F. Grease the loaf pan with butter.

2. **CREAM THE BUTTER AND SUGAR.** In the bowl of a stand mixer or in a large mixing bowl using an electric mixer, cream the butter and sugar together until light and fluffy, about 5 minutes. Add the eggs and vanilla, and beat to incorporate. Stir in the mashed bananas.

3. **COMBINE THE DRY INGREDIENTS.** In a medium mixing bowl, combine the flour, baking soda, and salt.

4. **COMBINE THE WET AND DRY INGREDIENTS.** Gently stir the dry mixture into the wet mixture until just combined. Fold in the nuts.

5. **BAKE THE BREAD.** Transfer the batter to the prepared loaf pan, smooth the top, and bake in the preheated oven for 55 to 60 minutes, until a wooden skewer or toothpick inserted into the center comes out clean.

6. **COOL AND SERVE.** Remove the pan from the oven and let it cool on a wire rack for several minutes. Remove the loaf from the pan and let it cool completely on the rack. Serve at room temperature.

GINGERBREAD COFFEE CAKE

IN A MUG

Prep time: 5 MINUTES   *Cook time:* 20 MINUTES   *Serves:* 1

LEVEL

NUT-FREE

EQUIPMENT
Large oven-safe coffee mug, whisk, small mixing bowl

FOR THE CAKE

2 tablespoons unsalted butter, melted

6 tablespoons all-purpose flour

2 tablespoons dark brown sugar

¼ teaspoon baking powder

¼ teaspoon ground ginger

⅛ teaspoon ground cinnamon

¼ cup (whole or low-fat) milk

1 tablespoon molasses

¼ teaspoon vanilla extract

FOR THE TOPPING

1 tablespoon unsalted butter, at room temperature

2 tablespoons all-purpose flour

1 tablespoon dark brown sugar

¼ teaspoon ground ginger

This delicious spiced cake is cooked *right in a coffee mug*. The best part? It takes only a few minutes to mix the ingredients, then you can bake and serve the cake in the mug. Easy peasy!

1. **PREHEAT THE OVEN AND PREPARE THE MUG.** Preheat the oven to 350°F. Pour the melted butter into a large, oven-safe mug. Swirl the butter around so it coats the bottom and sides of the mug.

2. **ADD THE DRY INGREDIENTS.** Whisk the flour, brown sugar, baking powder, ginger, and cinnamon into the butter in the cup.

3. **ADD THE WET INGREDIENTS.** Stir the milk, molasses, and vanilla into the mug.

4. **MAKE THE STREUSEL TOPPING.** In a small mixing bowl, stir together the butter, flour, brown sugar, and ginger. Sprinkle the mixture over the batter in the mug.

5. **BAKE THE CAKE AND SERVE.** Bake the cake in the preheated oven for 15 to 20 minutes, until the cake is set. Serve warm.

Tip

Go to Mug Cakes in the Microwave (page 105) to find out how to use the microwave to cook up your mug cake in just a couple of minutes.

CHOCOLATE ZUCCHINI BREAD

Prep time: 15 MINUTES, PLUS 15 MINUTES TO REST   *Cook time:* 60 MINUTES   *Makes:* 1 LOAF

LEVEL 1

NUT-FREE

EQUIPMENT
9-by-5-by-3-inch loaf pan, medium mixing bowl, large mixing bowl, whisk, wooden skewer or toothpick

Nonstick cooking spray or butter, for greasing

1 cup all-purpose flour

½ cup unsweetened cocoa powder

1 teaspoon baking soda

¼ teaspoon salt

½ teaspoon ground cinnamon

2 eggs

¾ cup granulated sugar

½ cup (1 stick) unsalted butter, melted

1 teaspoon vanilla extract

¾ pound zucchini, grated and drained in a colander

Chocolate Zucchini Bread is the most brilliant invention. It's loaded with zucchini, which makes it incredibly moist, and honestly, no one will ever know there's something good for them in each chocolatey bite. Your Saturday morning breakfast or afterschool snack just became a whole lot healthier.

1. **PREHEAT THE OVEN AND PREPARE THE PAN.** Preheat the oven to 350°F. Grease the loaf pan with cooking spray or butter.

2. **MIX THE DRY INGREDIENTS.** In a medium mixing bowl, stir together the flour, cocoa powder, baking soda, salt, and cinnamon.

3. **COMBINE THE REMAINING INGREDIENTS.** In a large mixing bowl, whisk together the eggs, sugar, butter, and vanilla. Add the dry mixture to the wet mixture, and stir to combine. Gently stir in the zucchini.

4. **BAKE THE BREAD.** Transfer the batter to the prepared loaf pan and bake in the preheated oven for 50 to 60 minutes, until a wooden skewer or toothpick inserted into the center comes out clean.

5. **COOL AND SERVE.** Set the loaf pan on a wire rack to cool for 15 minutes, then remove the loaf from the pan and let cool on the rack. Slice and serve warm or at room temperature.

Tip

This bread will keep for up to 4 days tightly wrapped in plastic wrap. It can also be frozen, tightly wrapped in plastic wrap, for up to 3 months. Thaw on the countertop overnight, and slice just before serving.

CINNAMON RAISIN BREAD

Prep time: 20 MINUTES, PLUS 1 HOUR AND 40 MINUTES TO RISE AND 15 MINUTES TO COOL

Cook time: 50 MINUTES   *Makes:* 1 LOAF

LEVEL

NUT-FREE

EQUIPMENT

Medium mixing bowl, 3 large mixing bowls, electric mixer, clean dish towel, 9-by-5-by-3-inch loaf pan, rolling pin, small mixing bowl, pastry brush

FOR THE BREAD

1 cup warm whole
milk, divided

1 envelope (2¼ teaspoons)
active dry yeast

⅓ cup unsalted
butter, melted

⅓ cup granulated sugar

¼ cup sour cream

2 eggs, lightly beaten,
divided (1 for the dough and
1 for an egg wash)

3½ to 4 cups all-purpose
flour, divided

1 teaspoon salt

¾ cup raisins

Nonstick cooking spray

*(Ingredients continue on
next page).*

I love eating this cinnamon-scented bread when it's warm with a smear of creamy butter. It also makes the best toast later on, and—even better—French toast. Drizzle with maple syrup and serve with a few slices of bacon, and you'll have a fantastic breakfast.

1. PROOF THE YEAST. In a medium mixing bowl, combine ¾ cup of milk and the yeast. Set aside for about 10 minutes, until the mixture becomes foamy.

2. COMBINE THE WET INGREDIENTS. In a large mixing bowl, combine the melted butter, sugar, sour cream, 1 egg, and the remaining ¼ cup of milk.

3. COMBINE THE DRY INGREDIENTS AND MAKE THE DOUGH. In a separate large mixing bowl, stir together 3½ cups of flour and the salt. Add half of the flour mixture to the butter mixture, and mix with an electric mixer until well combined. Add the yeast mixture, and beat on low until just incorporated. Add the remaining flour mixture and the raisins, and beat on medium speed until the mixture is well combined and forms a smooth dough, about 4 minutes. If the dough is too sticky, add the remaining ½ cup of flour, a tablespoon or two at a time, as needed.

4. LET THE DOUGH RISE. Coat a large bowl lightly with cooking spray. Form the dough into a ball and put it in the greased bowl, turning once to coat all over with the spray. Cover the bowl with a clean dish towel, and set it in a warm spot on your countertop, until the dough has doubled in size, about 1 hour. »

FOR THE FILLING

½ cup brown sugar

2½ teaspoons ground cinnamon

½ cup unsalted butter, at room temperature

5. FORM THE LOAF AND MAKE THE FILLING. Spray the loaf pan with cooking spray. Turn the dough out onto a lightly floured work surface and knead it a few times. Cover with a dish towel and let rest for about 5 minutes. Using a rolling pin, roll out the dough into a 9-by-24-inch rectangle. In a small mixing bowl, mix together the brown sugar, cinnamon, and butter. Spread the butter mixture onto the rectangle of dough, covering all but about a 1-inch border on one of the short sides. With the fully covered short side nearest you, roll the dough up away from your body into a thick, 9-inch-long log. Pinch along the edge of the dough to seal the seam. Place the loaf seam-side down in the prepared loaf pan. Brush the top with the remaining beaten egg, and set the pan in a warm spot on your countertop and let rise for 30 minutes.

6. BAKE THE BREAD. Preheat the oven to 375°F. Bake the loaf for 40 to 50 minutes, until the top is golden brown and the bread is puffed and a wooden skewer or toothpick inserted into the center comes out clean.

7. COOL AND SERVE. Remove from the oven and set the loaf pan on a wire rack to cool for about 15 minutes. Remove the bread from the pan and slice to serve. Serve warm, at room temperature, or toasted.

Tips

You can prepare this bread through step 5, then cover with plastic wrap and refrigerate overnight. Bring to room temperature by letting it sit on the countertop for 30 minutes or so, then bake as directed.

This freezes really well. Slice the loaf and transfer the slices to individual freezer-safe resealable plastic bags. Store them in the freezer for up to 3 months. You'll be able to grab a slice or two any time you want and pop the frozen slices right into the toaster!

PUMPKIN SPICE BREAKFAST BREAD PUDDING

Prep time: 15 MINUTES   *Cook time:* 30 MINUTES   *Serves:* 6

LEVEL **1**

NUT-FREE

EQUIPMENT
8-inch square baking dish, large mixing bowl, whisk

1½ cups half-and-half

1 cup canned pumpkin purée (not pie filling)

½ cup granulated sugar

2 eggs plus 2 egg yolks

¼ teaspoon salt

1 teaspoon pumpkin pie spice

5 cups cubed (1-inch) day-old bread (such as baguette or French loaf)

This is one of those indulgent recipes that straddles the line between breakfast and dessert. It is the perfect thing to enjoy with your friends the morning after a fall sleepover, but since it uses canned pumpkin purée, you can really make it any time of year.

1. **PREHEAT THE OVEN AND PREPARE THE PAN.** Preheat the oven to 350°F. Have your baking dish ready. No need to grease it.

2. **COMBINE THE INGREDIENTS.** In a large mixing bowl, whisk together the half-and-half, pumpkin purée, sugar, eggs, egg yolks, salt, and pumpkin pie spice. Add the bread cubes to the pumpkin mixture, and toss to coat.

3. **BAKE THE BREAD PUDDING AND SERVE.** Transfer the mixture to the baking dish and bake in the preheated oven for 25 to 30 minutes, until the custard is set and the pudding is golden brown on top. Serve warm.

 Tip

Make individual bread puddings! Place 6 (8-ounce) ramekins on a baking sheet. Divide the mixture evenly between the ramekins and bake for about 15 minutes, until the custard is set and the pudding is golden brown on top.

FRUIT AND YOGURT MINI TARTS
WITH GRANOLA CRUST

Prep time: 15 MINUTES, PLUS 10 MINUTES TO COOL   *Cook time:* 15 MINUTES   *Makes:* 12 TARTS

LEVEL 1

GLUTEN-FREE

EQUIPMENT
*Standard 12-cup muffin tin,
medium mixing bowl*

Nonstick cooking spray

FOR THE CRUST

1 cup gluten-free
old-fashioned rolled oats

⅓ cup unsweetened
shredded coconut (optional)

¼ cup chopped pecans

¼ cup brown sugar

1 teaspoon ground cinnamon

Pinch salt

2 tablespoons unsalted
butter, melted

FOR THE FILLING

3 cups vanilla Greek yogurt

2 cups mixed berries or
other fruit

These beautiful tarts turn an everyday breakfast into a gorgeous work of art. Make the crusts over the weekend or the night before, and they become an easy school day breakfast. Fill them with yogurt and fruit just before serving.

1. **PREHEAT THE OVEN AND PREPARE THE PAN.** Preheat the oven to 350°F. Grease the muffin tin with cooking spray.

2. **COMBINE THE CRUST INGREDIENTS.** In a medium mixing bowl, combine the oats, coconut (if using), pecans, brown sugar, cinnamon, and salt, and stir to mix well. Add the butter and stir to combine.

3. **BAKE THE CRUSTS.** Spoon about 2 tablespoons of the granola mixture into each well of the prepared muffin tin, and press the granola down into the well so it covers the bottom and comes about a third of the way up the sides. Bake in the preheated oven for 10 minutes. Remove from the oven and use a spoon or the bottom of a juice glass to press the granola mixture firmly into the cups again. Return the tin to the oven and bake until the crusts are golden brown, 2 to 3 minutes more. Place the pan on a wire rack and let cool for 10 minutes. Slide a knife around the outside of each of the crusts to loosen it from the tin and then carefully lift it out. Cool the crusts completely on the wire rack.

4. **ASSEMBLE THE TARTS.** Just before serving, fill each crust with about ¼ cup of yogurt and top with the berries or other fruit.

Tip

You can make the crusts through step 3 and store them in an airtight container at room temperature for up to a week or in the freezer for up to 3 months. Thaw overnight at room temperature, and fill the tarts just before serving.

FLAKY BUTTERMILK BISCUITS

WITH HONEY BUTTER

Prep time: 15 MINUTES   *Cook time:* 15 MINUTES   *Makes:* 12 BISCUITS

LEVEL

NUT-FREE

EQUIPMENT

Medium mixing bowl, whisk, pastry cutter (or a fork or two knives), 3-inch round cookie cutter baking sheet, pastry brush, medium mixing bowl or stand mixer, rubber spatula

FOR THE BISCUITS

3 cups all-purpose flour

1½ tablespoons granulated sugar

1½ teaspoons salt

1 tablespoon baking powder

¾ teaspoon baking soda

¾ cup (1½ sticks) cold, unsalted butter, cut into ½-inch pieces, plus 2 tablespoons melted, for brushing, divided

1 cup plus 2 tablespoons buttermilk

FOR THE HONEY BUTTER

½ cup (1 stick) unsalted butter, at room temperature

2 tablespoons honey

Pinch salt

Biscuits are so easy to make from scratch—don't even think about buying a boxed mix. The honey butter in this recipe makes them even better. These pair nicely with bacon and eggs, or you can enjoy them all by their buttery selves.

1. **PREHEAT THE OVEN.** Preheat the oven to 400°F.

2. **MIX THE DRY INGREDIENTS.** In a medium mixing bowl, whisk together the flour, sugar, salt, baking powder, and baking soda to combine well.

3. **CUT IN THE BUTTER.** Using a pastry cutter, fork, or two knives, cut the butter pieces into the dry ingredients until the mixture forms pea-size lumps. Add the buttermilk and, using your hands, quickly mix it into the dry ingredients until the mixture comes together in a sticky dough.

4. **CUT AND BAKE THE BISCUITS.** On a lightly floured work surface, pat the dough out until it is about half an inch thick, then fold it over itself. Pat the dough out and fold it over 2 or 3 more times. Finally, pat the dough out into an even ¾-inch thickness and cut into biscuits using your cookie cutter. Arrange the biscuits on an ungreased baking sheet. Brush the melted butter over the tops of the biscuits. Bake in the preheated oven for 13 to 15 minutes, until the biscuits are puffed and golden brown on the outside.

5. MAKE THE HONEY BUTTER AND SERVE. In a medium mixing bowl or the bowl of a stand mixer, beat the butter on medium speed until it is smooth and creamy, about 2 minutes. Add the honey and salt and beat, scraping down the sides of the bowl with a rubber spatula as needed, until the mixture is well combined. Serve the biscuits warm with the honey butter.

Freeze unbaked biscuits for up to 3 months. After cutting them out, place them in a single layer on a baking sheet and freeze until frozen solid. Transfer to a freezer-safe resealable plastic bag. To bake, place frozen biscuits on a baking sheet and bake as directed above, adding a minute or two to the baking time.

HOMEMADE CROISSANTS

Prep time: 40 MINUTES, PLUS ABOUT 6.5 HOURS TO CHILL AND RISE AND 4 HOURS OR OVERNIGHT TO CHILL
Cook time: 20 MINUTES   *Makes:* 24 CROISSANTS

LEVEL

NUT-FREE

EQUIPMENT

Large mixing bowl or bowl of stand mixer, large resealable plastic bag, rolling pin, large baking sheet, plastic wrap, sharp knife or pizza cutter, clean dish towel, small mixing bowl, whisk

FOR THE DOUGH

¼ cup plus 2 tablespoons warm water

1½ tablespoons (2 envelopes) active dry yeast

¼ cup granulated sugar, divided

2 cups (4 sticks) unsalted butter, at room temperature

2 cups (whole or low-fat) milk

¼ cup (½ stick) unsalted butter, melted

1 tablespoon salt

5 cups all-purpose flour, divided, plus more for dusting and sprinkling

FOR THE EGG WASH

2 egg yolks

2 tablespoons water

Here is a recipe for the weekend baking warrior. It's not that hard, but it takes a lot of time so be aware of this before you start. The most difficult part is rolling out the dough and chilling it repeatedly (that's how those delectable flaky layers are formed—no shortcuts here). Stick it out, though, and I guarantee you'll impress your friends and yourself!

1. PROOF THE YEAST. In a large mixing bowl or the bowl of a stand mixer, combine the warm water, yeast, and a pinch of sugar. Let stand for about 10 minutes, until the mixture becomes foamy.

2. ROLL OUT THE BUTTER. While the yeast is proofing, put the room-temperature butter in a large, resealable plastic bag. Squeeze out as much air as possible before sealing. Using a rolling pin, flatten the butter into a 6-by-8-inch slab. Put the butter slab in the freezer for about 1 hour, until firm (this is about how long it will take to finish making the dough and chill it.)

3. FINISH MAKING THE DOUGH. Add the remaining sugar and the milk, melted butter, and salt to the yeast mixture, and mix well. Add ½ cup of flour, and beat by hand or with the mixer until well combined. Add the remaining flour ½ cup at a time, mixing after each addition, until the mixture comes together in a sticky dough.

4. ROLL OUT AND CHILL THE DOUGH. Place the dough on a lightly floured work surface, and sprinkle a bit of flour over the top. Using the rolling pin, roll out the dough into a 10-by-16-inch rectangle about half an inch thick. Place the dough on a large baking sheet, cover with plastic wrap, and chill in the refrigerator for about 45 minutes.

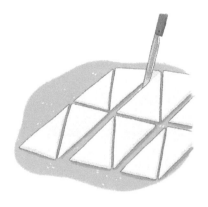

5. ADD THE BUTTER LAYER TO THE DOUGH. Place the dough on a lightly floured work surface with the long side facing you. Remove the butter from the plastic bag and place it in the center of the dough rectangle with the short side of the butter slab facing you. Fold each side of the dough over the butter like you are folding a letter. Pinch the edges of the dough to seal in the butter all the way around. Cover with plastic wrap and chill for 30 minutes.

6. CREATE THOSE FLAKY LAYERS. Once the dough has chilled, roll the dough out again into a 10-by-16-inch rectangle. Fold the rectangle again into thirds (again, as you would fold a letter), wrap it in plastic wrap, and chill for another 30 minutes. Repeat this rolling, folding, chilling process 3 more times. Finally, chill the dough for 4 hours or overnight.

7. FORM THE ROLLS AND LET THEM RISE. Work with half of the dough at a time (rewrap the other half and keep it in the refrigerator while you work with the first half). Place the dough on a lightly floured work surface, and sprinkle a bit of flour over the top. Roll out the dough into a 9-by-18-inch rectangle. Using a sharp knife or a pizza cutter, cut the dough in half lengthwise so you have 2 (4½-by-18-inch) strips. Cut each strip into 6 (3-by-4½-inch) rectangles, then cut each rectangle into 2 triangles by making a diagonal cut through the middle. With the short side of the triangle facing you, roll the dough away from your body, stretching the sides out a bit as you go. Place the rolls on a baking sheet, tucking the tip of the triangle underneath each roll and leaving 2 to 3 inches between the rolls. Cover with a clean dish towel and set the baking sheet in a warm place (about 75°F). Let rise for 2 to 3 hours, until doubled. »

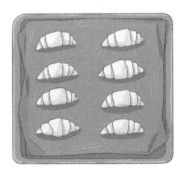

8. MAKE THE EGG WASH, BAKE THE CROISSANTS, AND SERVE.
Preheat the oven to 425°F. In a small bowl, whisk the egg yolks and water together to make the egg wash. Brush the egg wash over the tops of the croissants. Bake in the preheated oven for 15 to 18 minutes, until the croissants are golden brown. If you are baking more than one sheet pan full, bake them one sheet at a time. Remove the baking sheet from the oven, and place it on a wire rack. Serve warm or at room temperature.

Tips

You'll be using your refrigerator and freezer for this recipe, so before you start, make sure there is room for the baking sheet of dough and the butter.

Croissants are best eaten the day they are baked, but you can freeze them—unbaked—for up to 3 months. Follow the recipe instructions through step 7. Cover the baking sheet with plastic and freeze. Once frozen, you can transfer the unbaked croissants to a freezer-safe resealable plastic bag. To bake, thaw the croissants overnight in the refrigerator and bake as instructed in the recipe.

MAPLE-PECAN MORNING BUN BREAKFAST CAKE

Prep time: 20 MINUTES   *Cook time:* 35 MINUTES   *Serves:* 12

LEVEL 1

EQUIPMENT

9-by-13-inch baking pan, large mixing bowl, electric mixer or wooden spoon, small mixing bowl, rubber spatula (or knife), toothpick

FOR THE CAKE

½ cup unsalted butter, melted, plus more for greasing

½ cup granulated sugar

2 eggs

½ cup maple syrup

2 teaspoons vanilla extract

3 cups all-purpose flour

4 teaspoons baking powder

¼ teaspoon salt

1½ cups (whole or low-fat) milk

FOR THE TOPPING

1 cup (2 sticks) unsalted butter, melted

1 cup brown sugar

½ cup finely chopped pecans

2 tablespoons all-purpose flour

1 tablespoon ground cinnamon

¼ cup maple syrup

I absolutely adore morning buns, but they take a lot of time to make. This quick coffee cake captures all the morning bun flavors in an easy-to-make cake that can be ready in under an hour.

1. **PREHEAT THE OVEN AND PREPARE THE BAKING PAN.** Preheat the oven to 350°F. Grease the baking pan with butter.

2. **MIX THE CAKE INGREDIENTS.** In a large mixing bowl, using an electric mixer or a wooden spoon, cream together the butter and sugar until fluffy, about 5 minutes. Add the eggs, maple syrup, and vanilla, and beat to combine. Add the flour, baking powder, and salt, and stir to mix well. Stir in the milk. Transfer the batter to the prepared baking pan.

3. **MAKE THE TOPPING.** In a small mixing bowl, stir together the melted butter, brown sugar, pecans, flour, and cinnamon. Spread the topping mixture over the batter in the baking pan, using a rubber spatula (or knife) to swirl it into the batter.

4. **BAKE THE COFFEE CAKE.** Bake in the preheated oven for 30 to 35 minutes, until a toothpick inserted into the center comes out clean.

5. **TOP AND SERVE.** Remove from the oven and drizzle the maple syrup over the top while the cake is still hot. Serve warm or let cool to room temperature before serving.

 Tip

Cut the cake into large slices and wrap individually in plastic wrap. The slices will keep this way for several days.

4

COOKIES, BROWNIES, and BARS

Cookies, brownies, and bars are often the first things new bakers make when they dive into the wonderful world of flour, sugar, and butter . . . and for good reason! They're easy to make, they're hard to mess up, and everyone loves them. Bring a container of homemade cookies to your study group. Share the fudgy brownies you made at band practice. Whip up a batch of cheesecake bars to bring to your next movie night. Trust me, you'll be a hero! Have leftovers? See pages 38 to 39 for storage instructions.

CHOCOLATE MINT CHIP COOKIES

Prep time: 10 MINUTES, PLUS 5 MINUTES TO COOL *Cook time:* 25 MINUTES *Makes:* ABOUT 30 COOKIES

LEVEL 1

NUT-FREE

EQUIPMENT
2 baking sheets, parchment paper, medium mixing bowl, large mixing bowl with electric mixer or stand mixer

2½ cups all-purpose flour

¾ cup unsweetened cocoa powder

1 teaspoon baking soda

½ teaspoon salt

1 cup (2 sticks) unsalted butter, at room temperature

1 cup granulated sugar

1 cup brown sugar

1 teaspoon vanilla extract

2 eggs, at room temperature

1 (10-ounce) package mint chocolate chips

Imagine these as a sort of reverse mint chip ice cream: a gooey, chocolatey cookie studded with mint chocolate chips. I like to use the green mint chocolate chips (which are actually white chocolate with mint flavoring) when I can find them because they make the cookies look so pretty, but you can use regular mint chocolate chips, too.

1. **PREHEAT THE OVEN AND PREPARE THE PANS.** Preheat the oven to 350°F. Line 2 baking sheets with parchment paper.

2. **COMBINE THE DRY INGREDIENTS.** In a medium mixing bowl, mix the flour, cocoa, baking soda, and salt.

3. **COMBINE THE WET AND DRY INGREDIENTS.** In the bowl of a stand mixer or in a large mixing bowl using an electric mixer, cream together the butter and both sugars until the mixture is light and fluffy, about 5 minutes. Add the vanilla and then the eggs one at a time, beating to incorporate after each addition. Add the flour mixture in 2 or 3 additions, beating until combined after each. Stir in the mint chocolate chips.

4. **BAKE AND SERVE THE COOKIES.** Drop the dough onto the prepared baking sheets in large spoonfuls, flattening each a bit with the back of the spoon. Leave about 2 inches of space between each cookie. Bake each sheet one at a time in the preheated oven for 10 to 12 minutes until the cookies are firm but remain a bit soft in the center. Remove the sheet from the oven and let cool on the baking sheet for 5 minutes before transferring the cookies to a wire rack to cool completely before serving.

FLOURLESS DOUBLE CHOCOLATE COOKIES

Prep time: 10 MINUTES   *Cook time:* 15 MINUTES   *Makes:* ABOUT 24 COOKIES

LEVEL

NUT-FREE
GLUTEN-FREE

EQUIPMENT
2 baking sheets, parchment paper, large mixing bowl, wooden spoon or rubber spatula, medium (1½ to 2 tablespoon) cookie scoop

2 cups confectioners' sugar

1¼ cups unsweetened cocoa powder

1 teaspoon espresso powder (optional)

½ teaspoon ground cinnamon

¼ teaspoon salt

3 eggs, lightly beaten

1½ teaspoons vanilla extract

5 ounces bittersweet chocolate chips

These fudgy little bites of heaven are rich and ultra-chocolatey, plus they're flourless, so they're perfect for people with a gluten allergy. With all this over-the-top chocolate goodness, be sure to serve them with a tall glass of cold milk.

1. PREHEAT THE OVEN AND PREPARE THE PANS. Preheat the oven to 350°F. Line 2 baking sheets with parchment paper.

2. COMBINE THE INGREDIENTS. In a large mixing bowl, stir together the sugar, cocoa powder, espresso powder (if using), cinnamon, and salt. Add the eggs, stirring with a wooden spoon or rubber spatula, until combined. Stir in the vanilla and fold in the chocolate chips.

3. BAKE AND SERVE THE COOKIES. Using your cookie scoop, drop the dough, 1½ inches apart, onto the prepared baking sheets. Bake both sheets of cookies at once in the preheated oven for 11 to 13 minutes, until the tops and edges begin to crack, rotating the pans halfway through baking. The center will still be a bit gooey. Set the baking sheets on a wire rack and let the cookies cool completely on the sheets before serving.

OATMEAL GINGERBREAD COOKIES

Prep time: 10 MINUTES   *Cook time:* 20 MINUTES   *Makes:* ABOUT 36 COOKIES

LEVEL **1**

NUT-FREE

EQUIPMENT
2 baking sheets, parchment paper, large mixing bowl with electric mixer or stand mixer, medium (1½ to 2 tablespoon) cookie scoop

½ cup (1 stick) unsalted butter, at room temperature

½ cup granulated sugar

½ cup brown sugar

¼ cup molasses

1 egg

1¼ cups all-purpose flour

¾ cup old-fashioned rolled oats

1 teaspoon baking soda

1 teaspoon ground ginger

¼ teaspoon ground cloves

¼ teaspoon salt

Spicy gingerbread meets classic chewy oatmeal cookie in a mashup that will quickly become one of your favorites. Pop a few into your lunch bag for a midday pick-me-up or enjoy them with a glass of milk to kick-start an afternoon study session.

1. PREHEAT THE OVEN AND PREPARE THE PAN. Preheat the oven to 375°F. Line 2 baking sheets with parchment paper.

2. CREAM THE BUTTER AND SUGAR. In the bowl of a stand mixer or in a large mixing bowl using an electric mixer, cream the butter with both sugars, beating on medium-high speed, until light and fluffy. Add the molasses and egg, and beat until just combined.

3. ADD THE DRY INGREDIENTS. Add the flour, oats, baking soda, ginger, cloves, and salt to the creamed butter mixture, and beat on medium speed just until well combined.

4. BAKE AND SERVE THE COOKIES. Scoop the dough onto the prepared baking sheets, pressing down slightly with the back of the scoop to flatten them a bit. Bake the sheets one at a time in the preheated oven for 10 minutes each. Set the baking sheets on a wire rack and let the cookies cool completely on the sheets before serving.

TO EAT THE COOKIE DOUGH OR NOT TO EAT THE COOKIE DOUGH . . .

The simple fact is that raw eggs can contain a bacteria called salmonella, which can make you sick. So it's not a good idea to eat raw cookie dough. You'll also want to wash bowls and utensils that have touched raw egg if using again to mix ingredients that won't be baked, like frosting. If you cook a contaminated egg in a recipe, the heat will kill the salmonella germs, making it safe to eat. That's why this isn't an issue with baked cookies.

There's an exception, though! You can buy pasteurized eggs in most supermarkets, which have been heated to a high enough temperature to destroy salmonella, so they are safe to eat raw. If you make your cookies with pasteurized eggs instead of regular eggs, you can safely lick the spoon all you like! And in case you were wondering, most commercially made cookie dough products are made with pasteurized eggs to avoid this very issue.

CINNAMON PINWHEEL COOKIES

Prep time: 30 MINUTES, PLUS ABOUT 2 HOURS TO CHILL THE DOUGH   *Cook time:* 15 MINUTES
Makes: ABOUT 48 COOKIES

LEVEL

EQUIPMENT

Large mixing bowl with electric mixer or stand mixer, plastic wrap, parchment paper, rolling pin, 2 baking sheets

FOR THE PLAIN DOUGH

½ cup confectioners' sugar

¾ cup (1½ sticks) unsalted butter, at room temperature

½ teaspoon salt

1½ teaspoons vanilla extract

1¼ cups all-purpose flour

FOR THE CINNAMON DOUGH

¾ cup (1½ sticks) unsalted butter

¼ cup plus 2 tablespoons brown sugar

½ teaspoon salt

½ teaspoon vanilla extract

1 tablespoon ground cinnamon

½ cup chopped pecans, finely ground in a food processor or blender

1¼ cups all-purpose flour, plus more for rolling

Sporting a spiral pattern of dark- and light-colored dough, these crunchy cinnamon- and vanilla-laced cookies are ideal for dunking in a glass of milk or hot chocolate. They look so festive that I always make a batch for the holiday cookie platter, and now you can, too.

1. **MAKE THE PLAIN COOKIE DOUGH.** In the bowl of a stand mixer or in a large mixing bowl using an electric mixer, cream together the sugar and butter until fluffy, about 5 minutes. Beat in the salt and vanilla. Add the flour, and beat to combine. Form the dough into a flat disk shape, wrap it in plastic wrap, and chill it in the refrigerator for at least 1 hour.

2. **MAKE THE CINNAMON DOUGH.** In the bowl of a stand mixer or in a large mixing bowl using an electric mixer, cream together the butter and sugar until fluffy, about 5 minutes. Beat in the salt and vanilla. Add the cinnamon, ground pecans, and flour, and beat to combine. Form the dough into a flat disk shape, wrap it in plastic wrap, and chill it in the refrigerator for at least 1 hour.

3. **ROLL OUT THE DOUGH.** Place a sheet of parchment paper on your work surface and lightly dust it with flour. Using a rolling pin, roll out the chilled plain dough on the parchment into a large rectangle, about 18 by 12 inches. Repeat with the cinnamon dough on another piece of parchment, making the cinnamon dough rectangle slightly smaller than the plain dough (17½ by 11½).

4. FORM THE COOKIES. Lay the cinnamon dough on top of the plain dough. Starting with one of the long sides, roll the dough up into a tight cylinder. Seal the edge, wrap in plastic wrap, and chill in the freezer for at least 45 minutes.

5. PREHEAT THE OVEN AND PREPARE THE PANS. Preheat the oven to 350°F. Line 2 baking sheets with parchment paper.

6. CUT, BAKE, AND SERVE THE COOKIES. Unwrap the chilled log of dough. Then, using a sharp or serrated knife, cut the log into ¼-inch-thick slices. Arrange the slices on the prepared cookie sheets. Bake both sheets together in the preheated oven for 12 to 14 minutes, until they are firm and just beginning to brown. Transfer the cookies to a wire rack to cool before serving.

CANDY BAR COOKIES

Prep time: 30 MINUTES, PLUS 1 HOUR TO CHILL THE DOUGH AND 30 MINUTES TO COOL
Cook time: 35 MINUTES *Makes:* ABOUT 36 COOKIES

LEVEL

NUT-FREE

EQUIPMENT
Food processor, large mixing bowl with electric mixer, or stand mixer; plastic wrap, sharp or serrated knife, baking sheet, medium microwave-safe bowl, small cookie scoop (or spoon)

1 cup (2 sticks) unsalted butter, at room temperature

½ cup confectioners' sugar

2 cups all-purpose flour

1 teaspoon vanilla extract

¼ teaspoon salt

14 soft caramel candies

1 tablespoon heavy (whipping) cream

1 (10-ounce) package milk chocolate chips

One of my favorite candy bars tastes like these fancy-looking layered cookies. Hint: If you know the one that has layers of shortbread cookie, caramel, and chocolate, you'll know what I'm talking about. They are adorable and easy to make, so I love baking these as a thoughtful little gift for someone special.

1. **MAKE THE SHORTBREAD DOUGH.** In a food processor, a large mixing bowl with an electric mixer, or the bowl of a stand mixer, cream the butter. Add the sugar and continue mixing until well combined. Add the flour, vanilla, and salt, and mix until the dough comes together in a smooth ball. Form the dough into a log about 12 inches long and about 2½ inches thick. Wrap the log tightly in plastic wrap and refrigerate for at least 1 hour.

2. **PREHEAT THE OVEN TO 300°F.**

3. **CUT THE SHORTBREAD BASES AND BAKE.** Remove the dough from the refrigerator and cut into ¼-inch-thick slices using a very sharp or serrated knife. Place the rounds half an inch apart on an ungreased baking sheet. Bake the cookies in the pre-heated oven for 25 to 30 minutes, until they are lightly golden. Transfer the baking sheet to a wire rack, and let the cookies cool on the sheet.

4. PREPARE THE CARAMEL LAYER. In a medium, microwave-safe bowl, combine the caramels and cream. Heat in the microwave for 1 minute. Remove the bowl from the microwave, stir the mixture, and heat for another 30 seconds. Stir until the mixture is well combined and smooth. Using a small cookie scoop or a spoon, drop about 1½ teaspoons of caramel on top of each cookie.

5. PREPARE THE CHOCOLATE LAYER AND SERVE. Place the chocolate chips in the microwave-safe bowl and heat for 1 minute. Remove the bowl from the microwave, stir, and heat for 30 seconds more. Stir until smooth. Spread about 1 teaspoon of the melted chocolate on top of the caramel layer on each cookie. Let the cookies cool for about 30 minutes until they are completely set before serving.

WHOOPIE PIES

Prep time: 30 MINUTES   *Cook time:* 10 MINUTES   *Makes:* ABOUT 20 PIES

LEVEL 2

NUT-FREE

EQUIPMENT
2 baking sheets, large mixing bowl with electric mixer or stand mixer, medium mixing bowl, whisk

FOR THE PIES

½ cup (1 stick) unsalted butter, at room temperature, plus more for greasing

1½ cups granulated sugar

2 eggs

¼ cup vegetable oil

1½ teaspoons vanilla extract

3 cups all-purpose flour

1 cup unsweetened cocoa powder

½ teaspoon baking powder

1 teaspoon baking soda

½ teaspoon salt

1½ cups (whole or low-fat) milk, divided

Whoopie pies are little mounds of chocolatey cake sandwiching a creamy marshmallow filling. Some say they originated in Maine in the 1920s, though people from Pennsylvania claim they baked them first. Wherever they come from, they have become quite popular from coast to coast. These indulgent sandwich cookies will please everyone from your younger siblings to your great-grandparents.

1. **PREHEAT THE OVEN AND PREPARE THE PANS.** Preheat the oven to 350°F. Grease 2 baking sheets with butter.

2. **MIX THE WET INGREDIENTS.** In the bowl of a stand mixer or in a large mixing bowl using an electric mixer, beat the butter, sugar, and eggs on medium speed to combine well. Add the oil and vanilla, and beat until incorporated.

3. **MAKE THE BATTER.** In a medium mixing bowl, whisk together the flour, cocoa, baking powder, baking soda, and salt. Add half of the dry mixture to the wet mixture, and beat to incorporate. Add ¾ cup of milk, and beat to combine. Add the remaining dry mix and the remaining ¾ cup of milk, and beat to combine.

4. **BAKE THE CAKES.** Drop the batter onto the prepared baking sheets by the teaspoonful, leaving about 2 inches of space in between. Bake both trays together in the preheated oven for 10 to 12 minutes, switching the position of the baking sheets halfway through cooking. Transfer the baking sheets from the oven to a wire rack to cool.

FOR THE FILLING

1½ cups (3 sticks) unsalted butter, at room temperature

2 cups confectioners' sugar

2 cups marshmallow cream topping (such as Marshmallow Fluff)

1 teaspoon vanilla extract

⅓ to ½ cup (whole or low-fat) milk

5. **MAKE THE FILLING AND FILL THE PIES.** In the bowl of a stand mixer or in a large mixing bowl using an electric mixer, beat together the butter, sugar, marshmallow cream, and vanilla until well combined. Add the milk, a little at a time, just until the mixture reaches a creamy, spreadable consistency (you may not need to use all of the milk). Spread the filling onto half of the cakes, then top with the remaining cakes to make sandwiches.

6. **SERVE OR STORE THE PIES.** Serve immediately or wrap the pies individually in plastic wrap and store in the refrigerator for up to 3 days or in the freezer for up to 3 months.

HOMEMADE MACARONS

Prep time: 1 HOUR, PLUS 30 MINUTES TO DRY   *Cook time:* 15 MINUTES   *Makes:* ABOUT 12 MACARONS

LEVEL 3

GLUTEN-FREE

EQUIPMENT
Baking sheet, parchment paper, sieve, 2 large mixing bowls, whisk, piping bag fitted with ½-inch tip

FOR THE MACARONS

1 cup almond flour
(or almond meal if you
can't find the flour)

1 cup confectioners' sugar

2 egg whites

Pinch salt

¼ cup granulated sugar

FOR THE FILLING

⅔ cup unsalted butter, at
room temperature

⅔ cup confectioners' sugar

Macarons, those colorful little French sandwich cookies that are all over Instagram (not to be confused with coconut macaroons), are easier to make than you think. Plus, they are endlessly versatile. Change the flavor and color of both the batter and the filling using flavored extracts and gel or paste food coloring—you only need ½ to 1 teaspoon of extract and a few drops of food coloring paste to create nearly endless varieties.

1. **PREPARE THE PAN.** Line a baking sheet with parchment paper.

2. **COMBINE THE DRY INGREDIENTS.** Using a sieve, sift the almond flour and confectioners' sugar into a large mixing bowl.

3. **WHISK THE EGG WHITES TO STIFF PEAKS.** In a separate large mixing bowl, whisk the egg whites with a pinch of salt until you can form soft peaks (see page 31). Add the granulated sugar a tablespoon at a time, whisking continuously, until the mixture is glossy, thick, and forms stiff peaks (see page 31). Fold in the almond flour mixture. Stir in any flavorings or colors (see headnote).

4. **PIPE THE COOKIES.** Transfer the mixture to a piping bag fitted with a ½-inch tip. Pipe ¾-inch circles onto the parchment paper on the baking sheet, leaving about 1 inch between each cookie. Tap the bottom of the baking sheet on the countertop a few times to release any air bubbles, then set aside to let them dry out for about 30 minutes.

5. PREHEAT THE OVEN. While the macarons are drying out, preheat the oven to 300°F

6. BAKE THE MACARONS. Bake in the preheated oven for 8 minutes. Open the door just a bit to release any steam, close it again, and continue to bake for 7 to 8 minutes more. Carefully slide the parchment paper onto a wire rack, and let the cookies cool completely before you try to lift them.

7. MAKE THE FILLING. In a mixing bowl, beat the butter until pale and fluffy, about 5 minutes. Add the confectioners' sugar a couple tablespoons at a time, beating thoroughly before adding the next bit of sugar. Add any flavoring extracts or food color paste to the mixture (see headnote), and beat to fully incorporate.

8. ASSEMBLE AND SERVE OR STORE THE MACARONS. Pipe or spoon the filling onto the flat side of half of the macarons, then top with the remaining cookies, pressing slightly to seal them together. Serve immediately or store in an airtight container in the refrigerator for up to 1 week.

RASPBERRY MELT-AWAYS

Prep time: 15 MINUTES, PLUS 30 MINUTES TO CHILL THE DOUGH AND 15 MINUTES TO SIT

Cook time: 20 MINUTES   *Makes:* ABOUT 36 COOKIES

LEVEL

NUT-FREE

EQUIPMENT

Baking sheet, parchment paper, large mixing bowl with electric mixer or stand mixer, plastic wrap, large cookie scoop or ice cream scoop, medium mixing bowl, fine-mesh sieve, whisk

---

FOR THE COOKIES

1 cup (2 sticks) unsalted butter, at room temperature

½ cup confectioners' sugar

½ teaspoon vanilla extract

½ teaspoon raspberry extract

1¼ cups all-purpose flour

½ cup cornstarch

¼ teaspoon salt

FOR THE GLAZE

½ cup fresh or frozen (thawed) raspberries

1 tablespoon granulated sugar

2 cups confectioners' sugar

½ teaspoon vanilla extract

1 to 2 tablespoons (whole or low-fat) milk

Sprinkles (optional)

These cookies literally melt away on your tongue thanks to the combination of confectioners' sugar and cornstarch in the dough. With a hint of raspberry flavor in the dough and a raspberry glaze, these fruit-forward cookies are a welcome addition to the usual cookie platter suspects. To make them extra special, add colorful or sparkly sprinkles over the glaze. Very pretty!

1. PREHEAT THE OVEN AND PREPARE THE PAN. Preheat the oven to 350°F. Line a baking sheet with parchment paper.

2. MAKE THE COOKIE DOUGH. In the bowl of a stand mixer or in a large mixing bowl using an electric mixer, beat the butter on medium speed until it is fluffy, about 1 minute. Add the confectioners' sugar, vanilla, and raspberry extract, and continue to beat until the mixture is well combined and creamy, about 3 more minutes. Add the flour, cornstarch, and salt, and beat on low until well combined. Cover the bowl with plastic wrap and chill in the refrigerator for 30 minutes. If the dough becomes too firm and hard to scoop, let it warm up a bit on the countertop until it is scoopable.

3. BAKE THE COOKIES. Using a large cookie scoop (or an ice cream scoop), scoop about 2 tablespoons of dough and form into a ball. Place the ball on the prepared baking sheet. Repeat with the rest of the dough, making sure to place the balls 2 inches apart on the baking sheet. Bake in the preheated oven for 16 to 18 minutes, until the edges are just beginning to brown. Let the cookies cool for 1 minute on the baking sheet, then transfer them to a wire rack to cool completely. »

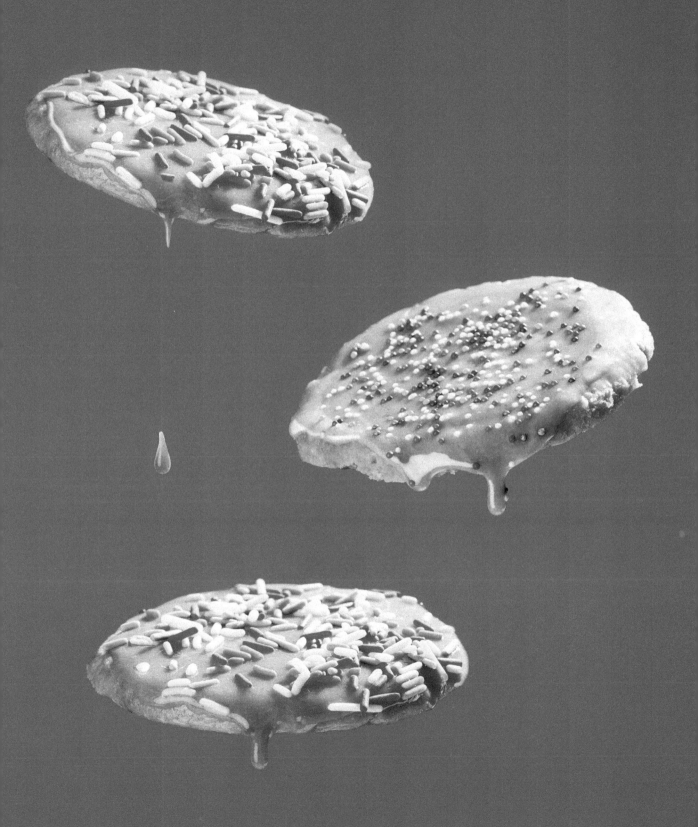

4. MAKE THE GLAZE. In a medium mixing bowl, stir together the raspberries and granulated sugar, mashing the berries up a bit with a fork. Let the mixture sit for about 15 minutes, until the berries release their juice. Strain the mixture through a fine-mesh sieve, pushing down on the berries to extract as much of the juice as possible. Discard the solids, and add the confectioners' sugar to the juice. Whisk until the mixture is smooth. Add the vanilla and 1 tablespoon of milk, and whisk to combine. Add additional milk as needed to get the glaze to a drizzling consistency.

5. FINISH AND SERVE THE COOKIES. Drizzle the glaze over the cooled cookies. Add sprinkles immediately (if using), before the glaze hardens, and serve.

LEMON BARS

Prep time: 15 MINUTES, PLUS 1 HOUR TO COOL AND 2 HOURS TO CHILL *Cook time:* 45 MINUTES
Makes: ABOUT 16 BARS

LEVEL

NUT-FREE

EQUIPMENT

9-inch square cake pan, parchment paper, 2 large mixing bowls with electric mixer or wooden spoon or stand mixer

FOR THE CRUST

Nonstick cooking spray

¾ cup (1½ sticks) unsalted butter, at room temperature

¼ cup plus 2 tablespoons granulated sugar

1½ cups all-purpose flour

⅛ teaspoon salt

FOR THE FILLING

1½ cups granulated sugar

¼ cup all-purpose flour

4 eggs

½ cup freshly squeezed lemon juice

⅓ cup confectioners' sugar, for garnish

Everyone loves a classic lemon bar with its buttery shortbread crust and tart-sweet lemon filling. The crust can be pressed right into the pan instead of rolling it out, which makes these amazingly easy to make. Take them to a party—and be prepared for lots of compliments.

1. PREHEAT THE OVEN AND PREPARE THE PAN. Preheat the oven to 350°F. Line the cake pan with enough parchment paper that it hangs a little over two ends, which will make it easy to lift the bars out of the pan after baking. Spray the paper and sides of the pan with cooking spray.

2. MAKE THE CRUST AND BAKE. In a large mixing bowl and using an electric mixer or wooden spoon, or in the bowl of a stand mixer, beat the butter until it is creamy and smooth. Add the sugar and beat until fluffy. Add the flour and salt, and beat on medium-low speed until well combined. Dump the mixture into the prepared cake pan and press it into an even layer. Bake in the preheated oven for 20 to 25 minutes, until it begins to turn golden on the edges. Remove from the oven, but leave the oven on.

3. MAKE THE FILLING AND BAKE. In a large mixing bowl, stir together the sugar and flour. Add the eggs and lemon juice, and stir to mix well. Pour the filling over the crust and bake in the preheated oven for 18 to 22 minutes, until the filling is set.

4. CHILL, GARNISH, AND SERVE. Remove the bars from the pan by lifting with the parchment paper edges. Transfer to a wire rack and let cool for 1 hour. Cover and chill in the refrigerator for at least 2 hours. Before serving, sprinkle the confectioners' sugar over the top and slice into bars or squares.

CHOCOLATE-CHERRY GRANOLA BARS

Prep time: 15 MINUTES, PLUS 15 MINUTES TO COOL   *Cook time:* 40 MINUTES   *Makes:* ABOUT 10 BARS

LEVEL

GLUTEN-FREE

EQUIPMENT

9-inch square cake pan, parchment paper; large rimmed baking sheet, large mixing bowl, small saucepan

Nonstick cooking spray

2 ½ cups gluten-free old-fashioned rolled oats

½ cup sliced almonds

½ cup honey

¼ cup unsalted butter

¼ cup brown sugar

¼ teaspoon salt

1 teaspoon vanilla extract

½ cup dried cherries

½ cup semisweet chocolate chips

I'm always searching for a granola bar that satisfies my sweet tooth while still qualifying as a "healthy" snack. I think you'll find that these fit the bill with a perfect combination of flavors and textures. They're sweetened mostly with honey and contain several nutrient-dense ingredients—oats, almonds, and dried cherries. It's a pretty simple recipe, so feel free to substitute your own favorite nuts, fruits, or other mix-ins.

1. **PREHEAT THE OVEN AND PREPARE THE PAN.** Preheat the oven to 350°F. Line the cake pan with parchment paper, leaving enough overhang to use as a sling to lift the finished bars out of the pan. Spray the paper and sides of the pan with cooking spray.

2. **TOAST THE OATS AND ALMONDS.** Spread the oats and almonds on a large, rimmed baking sheet and toast in the oven for 8 to 10 minutes. Transfer to a large mixing bowl. Leave the oven on.

3. **HEAT THE HONEY MIXTURE.** In a small saucepan set over medium heat, stir together the honey, butter, brown sugar, and salt and cook, stirring occasionally, until the butter is completely melted and the sugar is dissolved. Remove the pan from the heat, and stir in the vanilla.

4. **MIX TOGETHER THE HONEY MIXTURE AND OAT-NUT MIXTURE.** Pour the honey mixture over the oat-almond mixture in the bowl and stir to mix well. Stir in the cherries. Let it cool for at least 15 minutes before stirring in the chocolate chips.

5. **BAKE AND SERVE THE BARS.** Transfer the mixture to the prepared cake pan and, using wet hands, press it into an even layer. Bake for 25 to 30 minutes, until golden. Remove the pan from the oven and lift the bars out using the parchment paper sling. Cool on a wire rack, cut into bars, and serve.

RED VELVET CHEESECAKE BARS

Prep time: 15 MINUTES, PLUS 30 MINUTES TO COOL   *Cook time:* 30 MINUTES   *Makes:* 8 BARS

LEVEL

NUT-FREE

EQUIPMENT
8-inch square cake pan, large mixing bowl, medium mixing bowl, rubber spatula

FOR THE CAKE LAYER

½ cup (1 stick) unsalted butter, melted, plus more for greasing

1 cup granulated sugar

1 teaspoon vanilla extract

¼ cup unsweetened cocoa powder

Pinch salt

4 to 6 drops red food coloring gel

1 teaspoon white vinegar

2 eggs, lightly beaten

¾ cup all-purpose flour

FOR THE CHEESECAKE LAYER

8 ounces cream cheese, at room temperature

¼ cup granulated sugar

1 egg

½ teaspoon vanilla extract

Red velvet cake is rich and cocoa-flavored (with a slight tang from buttermilk or vinegar—sssh, don't tell!) and topped with a luscious cream cheese frosting. This twist on that classic cake adds a layered cheesecake batter to the red velvet flavor, transforming it into a beautiful bar. Make these when you get tired of the same old brownies.

1. **PREHEAT THE OVEN AND PREPARE THE PAN.** Preheat the oven to 350°F. Grease the cake pan with butter.

2. **MAKE THE CAKE LAYER.** In a large mixing bowl, stir together the melted butter and sugar. Add the vanilla, and stir to incorporate. Add the cocoa powder and salt, and stir to mix. Mix in the food coloring and vinegar. Add the eggs, and stir to mix. Gently fold in the flour just until combined. Transfer the batter to the prepared cake pan, reserving about ¼ cup to swirl into the cream cheese layer for visual effect.

3. **MAKE THE CHEESECAKE LAYER.** In a medium mixing bowl, beat together the cream cheese, sugar, egg, and vanilla. Spread this mixture over the cake layer in the cake pan, and smooth the top with a rubber spatula. Drop spoonfuls of the reserved cake batter onto the top and use the tip of a knife to create a swirling pattern.

4. **BAKE, COOL, AND SERVE.** Bake in the preheated oven for 30 minutes. Remove the pan from the oven and let cool completely on a wire rack for 30 minutes before cutting into bars and serving.

FUDGIEST BROWNIES

Prep time: 15 MINUTES   *Cook time:* 40 MINUTES   *Makes:* 16 BROWNIES

LEVEL 1

NUT-FREE

EQUIPMENT

9-inch square cake pan, parchment paper, large mixing bowl, sieve, rubber spatula

1 cup unsalted butter, melted and cooled

2 tablespoons vegetable oil

1 cup plus 2 tablespoons granulated sugar

1 cup plus 2 tablespoons brown sugar

4 eggs, at room temperature

1 tablespoon vanilla extract

1 teaspoon salt

1 cup all-purpose flour

1 cup unsweetened cocoa powder

4 ounces dark chocolate, coarsely chopped

Who doesn't love a deep, dark, chocolatey, fudgy brownie? Top with a scoop of vanilla ice cream and some hot fudge sauce, and you have a decadent dessert. Eat them plain and you'll still have an indulgent treat. If you love nuts, go ahead and add a handful.

1. **PREHEAT THE OVEN AND PREPARE THE PAN.** Preheat the oven to 350°F. Line the cake pan with parchment paper.

2. **MIX THE WET INGREDIENTS.** In a large mixing bowl, stir together the butter, oil, granulated sugar, and brown sugar. Stir in the eggs, vanilla, and salt, and mix to combine.

3. **ADD THE REMAINING INGREDIENTS.** Using a sieve, sift the flour and cocoa powder into the wet mixture. Then, using a rubber spatula, gently fold the mixture together until just combined. Stir in the chocolate.

4. **BAKE THE BROWNIES AND SERVE.** Pour the batter into the prepared cake pan, and smooth the top with a rubber spatula. Bake in the preheated oven for 35 to 40 minutes, just until the top is set. Remove the pan from the oven, and set it on a wire rack to cool. Cut into squares and serve.

COFFEE-TOFFEE BLONDIES

Prep time: 10 MINUTES   *Cook time:* 25 MINUTES   *Makes:* 16 BLONDIES

NUT-FREE

EQUIPMENT
8-inch square cake pan, large mixing bowl with an electric mixer or wooden spoon or stand mixer

½ cup (1 stick) unsalted butter, melted and cooled, plus more for greasing

1 cup dark brown sugar

1 egg

1 teaspoon vanilla extract

2 tablespoons espresso powder

Pinch salt

1 cup all-purpose flour

1 cup toffee chips

Blondies take the simplicity of brownies a step further. Instead of being flavored with chocolate, they get their distinctive butterscotch-y flavor from dark brown sugar, espresso powder, and toffee chips. Even chocolate gets boring sometimes, so these are a great alternative.

1. **PREHEAT THE OVEN AND PREPARE THE PAN.** Preheat the oven to 350°F. Grease the cake pan with butter.

2. **MAKE THE BATTER.** In a large mixing bowl and using an electric mixer or wooden spoon, or in the bowl of a stand mixer, beat together the butter and brown sugar until smooth. Add the egg and vanilla, and beat to combine. Add the espresso powder, salt, and flour, and mix completely. Stir in the toffee chips.

3. **BAKE AND SERVE THE BLONDIES.** Pour the batter into the prepared cake pan and bake for 20 to 25 minutes, until the middle is just set. Remove the pan from the oven and let cool on a wire rack before cutting into squares and serving.

5

CAKES, CUPCAKES,
and Cakes in a Jar

Cakes are the stuff of celebrations. Every birthday needs a cake, right? Where else are you going to put the candles? But cakes make great desserts whenever you feel like eating them. Most are pretty easy to make—all you need is a mixing bowl and one pan. Add a layer of frosting and, voilà, you're done! As you build your skills and baking experience, you can experiment with decorations and embellishments. No matter what kind of cake you decide to make, whomever you serve it to will be honored.

ANGEL FOOD CAKE

WITH RASPBERRY GLAZE

Prep time: 30 MINUTES, PLUS 2 HOURS TO COOL   *Cook time:* 45 MINUTES   *Serves:* 8 TO 10

LEVEL 3

NUT-FREE
DAIRY-FREE

EQUIPMENT

2 large mixing bowls, whisk, electric mixer or whisk, rubber spatula, tube pan or angel food cake pan, glass bottle (such as a soda, olive oil, or wine bottle), small mixing bowl, cake platter

FOR THE CAKE

1 cup all-purpose flour

1½ cups granulated sugar, divided

12 egg whites, at room temperature

½ teaspoon salt

1 teaspoon vanilla extract

1½ teaspoons cream of tartar

FOR THE GLAZE

1 cup confectioners' sugar

¼ cup fresh or frozen (thawed) raspberries

1 tablespoon freshly squeezed lemon juice, plus more if needed

Angel food cake is light, airy, and really flexible in terms of what you can flavor it with. It has a reputation for being finicky to make, but really the most difficult part is separating all those eggs (this recipe calls for 12!). If you aren't experienced with separating eggs (see page 30), make sure you have a few extra on hand just in case. Crack each egg into a small bowl first—if the yolk breaks, you won't taint the whole bowl of whites. After you've made this cake once, I guarantee you'll be an expert egg separator. I suggest you also make the Kiwi and Strawberry Tart with Vanilla Pastry Cream (page 124)—that recipe will use up some of the yolks you've separated.

1. **PREHEAT THE OVEN TO 325°F.**

2. **COMBINE THE DRY INGREDIENTS.** In a large mixing bowl, whisk the flour and ¾ cup of sugar together.

3. **WHIP THE EGG WHITES AND FOLD THE BATTER.** In a separate large mixing bowl, use the whisk or mixer to whip the egg whites, salt, and vanilla until the mixture becomes frothy. Sprinkle the cream of tartar over the top of the mixture. Continue whipping the mixture until it becomes glossy and forms stiff peaks (see page 31), a few minutes more. Add the remaining ¾ cup of sugar in 3 additions, whipping after each. Using a rubber spatula, gently fold in the flour-sugar mixture.

4. **BAKE THE CAKE.** Spoon the batter into the cake pan. Bake for 40 to 45 minutes. You know it's done when the top is light golden brown and springs back when you press on it.

5. LET COOL. Remove the cake from the oven and invert it over a bottle (so the bottle stands up in the cake pan hole and the cake is suspended upside down). Let cool for 2 hours.

6. MAKE THE GLAZE. In a small mixing bowl, stir together the confectioners' sugar, raspberries, and lemon juice, mashing the berries with a fork, until the mixture is very smooth. Add more lemon juice if needed to achieve a pourable consistency.

7. FINISH AND SERVE THE CAKE. Use a knife to loosen the edges of the cake from the pan, and transfer it to a cake platter. Pour the glaze over the top of the cake, cut into wedges, and serve.

Tip

Cream of tartar is an acidic powder (it's actually a by-product of the process of making grapes into wine) that acts as a stabilizer. When added to egg whites as you whip them, it helps the whipped foam hold its airy shape. You can find cream of tartar in the spice aisle of the supermarket.

DOUBLE-LAYER CARROT CAKE

WITH CREAM CHEESE FROSTING

Prep time: 30 MINUTES, PLUS 1½ HOURS TO COOL   *Cook time:* 35 MINUTES   *Serves:* 8 TO 10

LEVEL 3

NUT-FREE

EQUIPMENT

2 (9-inch) round cake pans, 2 large mixing bowls, wooden skewer or toothpick, large mixing bowl with electric mixer or stand mixer, cake platter, rubber spatula

FOR THE CAKE

Nonstick cooking spray

2 cups all-purpose flour

2 teaspoons baking powder

1 teaspoon baking soda

1½ teaspoons ground cinnamon

½ teaspoon ground ginger

¼ teaspoon ground nutmeg

½ teaspoon salt

¾ cup vegetable oil

4 eggs, at room temperature

1½ cups brown sugar

½ cup granulated sugar

½ cup crushed pineapple, drained

1 teaspoon vanilla extract

3 cups grated carrots

I love making carrot cake because I can pretend that it is healthy—it does have 3 cups of grated carrots in it! This cake is super moist with tons of flavor from the spices and pineapple. You can also add a cup of sweetened, shredded coconut to the batter for an extra kick.

1. PREHEAT THE OVEN AND PREPARE THE PANS. Preheat the oven to 350°F. Spray the cake pans with cooking spray.

2. COMBINE THE DRY INGREDIENTS. In a large mixing bowl, stir together the flour, baking powder, baking soda, cinnamon, ginger, nutmeg, and salt.

3. COMBINE THE WET INGREDIENTS. In another large mixing bowl, combine the oil, eggs, brown sugar, granulated sugar, pineapple, and vanilla, and stir or beat to mix well. Stir in the carrots.

4. COMBINE THE WET AND DRY INGREDIENTS. Stir the wet mixture into the dry mixture, and stir until just combined.

5. BAKE THE CAKE. Spoon the cake batter into the 2 prepared pans, dividing evenly. Bake in the preheated oven for 30 to 35 minutes, until a wooden skewer or toothpick inserted into the middle of the cake comes out clean. Remove the pans from the oven, and set them on a wire rack to cool for about 20 minutes. Run a knife around the edge of the pans to loosen the cakes from the sides, then invert them onto the wire rack. Let cool completely.

FOR THE CREAM CHEESE FROSTING

1 (8-ounce) package cream cheese, at room temperature

½ cup unsalted butter, at room temperature

2 cups confectioners' sugar

1 teaspoon vanilla extract

6. MAKE THE FROSTING. In the bowl of a stand mixer or in a large mixing bowl using an electric mixer, beat the cream cheese until smooth. Add the butter, and beat until smooth and well combined, about 1 minute. Add the confectioners' sugar and vanilla, and beat to combine.

7. ASSEMBLE, FROST, AND SERVE THE CAKE. Place one of the cake layers on a cake platter and, using a rubber spatula, spread about a third of the frosting over the top in a smooth layer. Place the second cake layer on top, and use the remaining frosting to frost the top and sides of the cake. Cut into wedges and serve.

Tip

Before you frost the cake, read about adding a crumb layer on page 36, where you'll find step-by-step instructions.

CREAM-FILLED CHOCOLATE LAYER CAKE

Prep time: 40 MINUTES, PLUS 6 HOURS TO COOL, SET, AND CHILL   *Cook time:* 55 MINUTES   *Serves:* 8 TO 10

LEVEL 3

NUT-FREE

EQUIPMENT

2 (9-inch) round cake pans, parchment paper, large heat-safe mixing bowl, medium mixing bowl, whisk, large mixing bowl with electric mixer or whisk or stand mixer, toothpick, 2 plates, small saucepan, medium microwave-safe bowl, rubber spatula

FOR THE CAKE

1 cup hot water

3 ounces semisweet chocolate, chopped

1 cup granulated sugar

1 cup brown sugar

1 cup sour cream

½ cup (1 stick) unsalted butter, at room temperature

2 large eggs

1½ teaspoons vanilla extract

2 cups all-purpose flour

½ cup unsweetened cocoa powder

2 teaspoons baking soda

1 teaspoon baking powder

¾ teaspoon salt

(Ingredients continue on next page)

This rich, chocolatey cake is filled with fluffy vanilla cream and then coated in a dark chocolate glaze. Basically, it's to die for! Don't be intimidated by the many different components. They are all easy to make. The key is leaving yourself enough time to do it all, and you'll be rewarded with a spectacular cake, worthy of a special birthday or other festive occasion.

1. PREHEAT THE OVEN AND PREPARE THE PANS. Preheat the oven to 350°F. Spray the cake pans with cooking spray, and dust them with a bit of cocoa powder or flour.

2. MELT THE CHOCOLATE. Place the chocolate in a small, heat-safe bowl and pour the hot water over the top. Let stand for 10 to 15 minutes while you prepare the rest of the batter. Stir the mixture with a fork until smooth.

3. MIX THE WET INGREDIENTS. In a large mixing bowl or in the bowl of a stand mixer, beat together the granulated and brown sugars, sour cream, and butter until fluffy and well combined. Add the eggs and vanilla and beat just to incorporate.

4. MIX THE DRY INGREDIENTS. In a medium mixing bowl, whisk together the flour, cocoa powder, baking soda, baking powder, and salt.

5. MIX THE WET AND DRY INGREDIENTS TOGETHER. Add the dry mixture to the wet mixture in several batches, mixing just to incorporate after each addition. »

FOR THE FILLING

1 cup (whole or low-fat) milk

5 tablespoons
all-purpose flour

1 teaspoon vanilla extract

1 cup (2 sticks)
unsalted butter

1 cup granulated sugar

FOR THE GLAZE

1 (12-ounce) bag semisweet
chocolate chips

1 cup heavy
(whipping) cream

1 tablespoon unsalted butter

2 tablespoons rainbow
sprinkles (optional)

6. BAKE THE CAKE. Pour the batter into the prepared cake pans, and bake in the preheated oven for 30 to 35 minutes, until a toothpick inserted into the center comes out clean. Remove the pans from the oven, and set them on a wire rack to cool completely. When completely cool, run a knife around the edges of the pans to loosen the cakes from the sides, then invert the cake layers onto plates.

7. MAKE THE FILLING. In a small saucepan, whisk the milk and flour together until there are no lumps. Set over medium-low heat and cook, stirring, until the mixture thickens, about 5 minutes. Remove the pan from the heat, and stir in the vanilla. In a large mixing bowl with an electric mixer or the bowl of a stand mixer set on medium-high speed, cream the butter and sugar together until it is pale and very fluffy, about 8 minutes. Add the milk mixture to the butter mixture, and continue to beat until the entire mixture is well combined and fluffy.

8. ASSEMBLE THE CAKE. Place one cake layer top-down on a parchment-lined wire rack. Spoon the cream filling on top, and smooth it into an even layer. Place the second cake layer top-down on top of the cream.

9. MAKE THE GLAZE. Put the chocolate chips, cream, and butter in a heat-safe bowl and microwave for 1 minute. Stir the mixture, and heat again in 30-second intervals, stirring in between, until the chocolate is completely melted and the mixture is smooth.

10. FINISH AND SERVE THE CAKE. Pour the glaze over the top of the cake, allowing it to spill over the edges and drip down so the entire cake is completely covered. Use a rubber spatula as needed to spread the glaze evenly over the sides and top, then garnish with the sprinkles. Let the glaze set for at least 1 hour, then transfer the cake to a serving plate. Refrigerate for at least 4 hours before serving chilled.

LEMON PUDDING CAKE

Prep time: 15 MINUTES   *Cook time:* 60 MINUTES   *Serves:* 6 TO 8

LEVEL 1

NUT-FREE

EQUIPMENT

8-inch square or round cake pan, large mixing bowl with electric mixer or stand mixer, large mixing bowl, whisk, rubber spatula

Butter, for greasing

4 eggs, at room temperature, separated

¾ cup sugar

½ cup unsalted butter, melted

1 teaspoon vanilla extract

¾ cup all-purpose flour

Zest of 1 lemon

¼ cup freshly squeezed lemon juice

1¾ cups (whole or low-fat) milk, warm but not hot

Confectioners' sugar, for garnish

This bright, lemony cake is like a magical science experiment. As the cake bakes, the batter separates into two distinct layers—cake on top and pudding on the bottom. Surprise and amaze your friends with this absolutely delicious feat of baking wizardry! It will make you look very accomplished.

1. **PREHEAT THE OVEN AND PREPARE THE PAN.** Preheat the oven to 325°F. Coat the cake pan with butter.

2. **WHIP THE EGG WHITES.** In the bowl of a stand mixer or in a large mixing bowl using an electric mixer, whip the egg whites until they form stiff peaks (see page 31).

3. **COMBINE THE BATTER.** In a separate large mixing bowl, whisk together the egg yolks and sugar until the mixture becomes pale. Add the melted butter and vanilla, and beat to combine. Add the flour, and mix until it is fully incorporated. Add the lemon zest and juice, and beat to mix. With the mixer running, add the milk. Using a rubber spatula, gently fold in the whipped egg whites, about one-third at a time, until they are mostly incorporated.

4. **BAKE THE CAKE.** Transfer the batter to the prepared cake pan, and bake in the preheated oven for 45 to 60 minutes, until the top is firm to the touch. Remove the cake pan from the oven, and let the cake cool completely on a wire rack. Sprinkle confectioners' sugar over the top, and serve at room temperature.

CHOCOLATE CHIP COOKIES AND MILK CAKE

Prep time: 45 MINUTES   *Cook time:* 35 MINUTES   *Serves:* 12

LEVEL 3

NUT-FREE

EQUIPMENT

2 (8-inch) round cake pans, medium mixing bowl, large mixing bowl with electric mixer or stand mixer, toothpick, cake platter, rubber spatula, piping bag and tip (optional)

FOR THE CAKE

Nonstick cooking spray

2¼ cups all-purpose flour

2 teaspoons baking powder

½ teaspoon salt

¾ cup unsalted butter

1¼ cups granulated sugar

3 eggs

1 tablespoon vanilla extract

1 cup (whole or low-fat) milk

⅓ cup sour cream

1¼ cups semisweet mini chocolate chips, plus more for decorating

This cake has all the flavors of chocolate chip cookies and a tall glass of cold milk. It's easy to make, and fun to serve. When I make this, I like to buy a bag of mini chocolate chip cookies and use them to decorate the outside of the cake.

1. **PREHEAT THE OVEN AND PREPARE THE PANS.** Preheat the oven to 350°F. Spray the cake pans with cooking spray.

2. **COMBINE THE DRY INGREDIENTS.** In a medium mixing bowl, stir together the flour, baking powder, and salt.

3. **CREAM THE BUTTER AND SUGAR.** In the bowl of a stand mixer or in a large mixing bowl using an electric mixer, cream the butter and sugar together until the mixture is light and fluffy, about 5 minutes. Add the eggs one at a time, beating to incorporate after each addition. Add the vanilla, and mix to incorporate.

4. **MAKE THE CAKE BATTER.** Add half of the flour mixture, and beat to combine. Add the milk and sour cream, and beat to combine. Add the remaining flour mixture, and mix well. Stir in the chocolate chips.

5. **BAKE THE CAKE.** Transfer the batter to the cake pans, dividing evenly. Bake in the preheated oven for 30 to 35 minutes, until a toothpick inserted into the center comes out clean. Remove the cakes from the oven, and set the pans on a wire rack to cool.

FOR THE FROSTING

⅔ cup unsalted butter

5 cups confectioners' sugar

1 tablespoon vanilla extract

5 to 6 tablespoons (whole or low-fat) milk

6. MAKE THE FROSTING. In the bowl of a stand mixer or in a large mixing bowl using an electric mixer, cream the butter and confectioners' sugar together until the mixture is thick and fluffy, about 5 minutes. Add the vanilla and then the milk 1 tablespoon at a time, mixing between each addition until you reach your desired consistency.

7. ASSEMBLE AND SERVE THE CAKE. Remove one of the cake layers from the pan, and set it on a cake platter. Using a rubber spatula, spread frosting over the top, smoothing it into an even layer. Add the second cake layer, and cover the top and sides with frosting. If you like, you can transfer any remaining frosting to a piping bag and pipe a decorative border around the top. Use chocolate chips to decorate the sides and top of the cake. Refrigerate. About 20 minutes before serving, remove the cake from the refrigerator to let it warm up a bit. Cut into wedges and serve.

Tip

Before you frost the cake, read about adding a crumb layer on page 36, where you'll find step-by-step instructions.

PEANUT BUTTER AND JELLY CUPCAKES

Prep time: 20 MINUTES   *Cook time:* 20 MINUTES   *Makes:* 18 CUPCAKES

LEVEL 3

EQUIPMENT

2 standard 12-cup muffin tins, 18 paper cupcake liners, large bowl with electric mixer or stand mixer, medium mixing bowl, whisk, piping bag and tip or apple corer, piping bag and tip or resealable plastic bag (optional)

FOR THE CUPCAKES

¼ cup (½ stick) unsalted butter, at room temperature

½ cup smooth peanut butter

⅔ cup brown sugar

2 eggs

⅔ cup (whole or low-fat) milk

2 teaspoons vanilla extract

2 cups all-purpose flour

2 teaspoons baking powder

½ teaspoon salt

1½ cups fruit jelly (strawberry, raspberry, or grape), at room temperature

Everybody's favorite sandwich meets everybody's favorite tiny cakes! There is no better party treat than these, with their smooth peanut butter frosting and sweet fruit jelly filling. You can actually use any type of fruit paste in these: jelly, jam, preserves, or even marmalade. Whatever suits your fancy.

1. PREHEAT THE OVEN AND PREPARE THE PANS. Preheat the oven to 350°F and insert 18 paper liners into the muffin tins. It's okay that there will be 6 empty muffin cups.

2. COMBINE THE WET INGREDIENTS. In the bowl of a stand mixer or in a large mixing bowl using an electric mixer, cream together the butter, peanut butter, and sugar until the mixture is pale and fluffy, about 5 minutes. Add the eggs one at a time, beating well after each addition. Add the milk and vanilla, and beat to incorporate.

3. COMBINE THE DRY INGREDIENTS. In a medium mixing bowl, whisk together the flour, baking powder, and salt. Add the dry mixture to the wet mixture in 2 or 3 additions, beating just to incorporate after each addition.

4. BAKE THE CUPCAKES. Scoop the batter into the prepared muffin tins, filling each cup about two-thirds full. Bake in the preheated oven for 15 to 18 minutes, until a toothpick inserted into the center comes out clean. Remove the tins from the oven, and set on a wire rack to cool completely.

5. FILL THE CUPCAKES. You can use a piping bag fitted with a plain round tip to fill the cupcakes with the jelly by poking the tip into the center of the cupcake. If you don't have a piping bag, use an apple corer to remove the center of the cupcake so you have a well in the middle, and spoon jelly into the well.

FOR THE FROSTING

½ cup smooth peanut butter

½ cup (1 stick) unsalted butter, at room temperature

2 teaspoons vanilla extract

2 cups confectioners' sugar

1 to 3 tablespoons (whole or low-fat) milk

6. MAKE THE FROSTING. In the bowl of a stand mixer or in a large mixing bowl using an electric mixer, cream together the peanut butter, butter, and vanilla until the mixture is light and fluffy, about 3 minutes. Add the confectioners' sugar along with 2 tablespoons of milk, and beat until smooth. Add the milk 1 tablespoon at a time as needed to achieve a spreadable consistency.

7. DECORATE THE CUPCAKES. Using a piping bag fitted with a plain or star-shaped tip, pipe the frosting onto the cupcakes in an outside-in spiral (see page 36), leaving an indentation in the center. If you don't have a piping bag, you can use a resealable plastic bag with one of the corners snipped off, or simply spread the frosting onto the cupcakes with a knife. Spoon a bit of jelly into each indentation for decoration and serve.

Tip

Make sure your cupcakes are completely cooled before you attempt to frost them. If they're still warm, you'll end up with drooping frosting that's full of cake crumbs.

ESPRESSO-MOCHA CUPCAKES

WITH BUTTERCREAM FROSTING

Prep time: 20 MINUTES *Cook time:* 20 MINUTES *Makes:* 18 CUPCAKES

LEVEL

NUT-FREE

EQUIPMENT

2 standard 12-cup muffin tins, 18 paper cupcake liners, large mixing bowl with electric mixer or stand mixer, medium mixing bowl, whisk, toothpick, small mixing bowl, piping bag and tip or resealable plastic bag (optional)

FOR THE CUPCAKES

½ cup (1 stick) unsalted butter, at room temperature

½ cup granulated sugar

½ cup brown sugar

1 egg, at room temperature

½ cup brewed coffee, at room temperature

½ cup (whole or low-fat) milk

1 teaspoon vanilla extract

1⅓ cups all-purpose flour

⅓ cup unsweetened cocoa powder

1½ teaspoons espresso powder

1 teaspoon baking powder

½ teaspoon baking soda

¼ teaspoon salt

Coffee enhances chocolate, and chocolate complements coffee, making this one of the best flavor combinations on earth. These chocolatey cupcakes pack a triple coffee punch—there is both brewed coffee and espresso powder in the cupcakes, as well as espresso powder in the buttercream. If you eat these before a study session, I guarantee you'll be perked up. There will be no cat naps!

1. PREHEAT THE OVEN AND PREPARE THE PANS. Preheat the oven to 350°F. Put 18 paper liners in the muffin tins. It's okay that there will be 6 empty muffin cups.

2. COMBINE THE WET INGREDIENTS. In the bowl of a stand mixer or in a large mixing bowl using an electric mixer, cream together the butter and both sugars until the mixture is light and fluffy, about 5 minutes. Add the egg, brewed coffee, milk, and vanilla, and beat to combine.

3. COMBINE THE DRY INGREDIENTS. In a medium mixing bowl, whisk together the flour, cocoa powder, espresso powder, baking powder, baking soda, and salt. With the electric mixer set on low, add the dry mixture to the wet mixture, one-third at a time, beating just to incorporate after each addition.

4. BAKE THE CUPCAKES. Scoop the batter into the prepared muffin tins, filling each cup about two-thirds full. Bake in the preheated oven for 18 to 20 minutes, until a toothpick inserted into the center comes out clean. Remove the tins from the oven, and place them on a wire rack to let the cupcakes cool completely.

FOR THE FROSTING

1 cup (2 sticks) unsalted butter, at room temperature

2½ cups confectioners' sugar

1½ teaspoons vanilla extract

1½ teaspoons espresso powder

18 chocolate-covered espresso beans, for decorating (optional)

5. MAKE THE FROSTING. In the bowl of a stand mixer or in a large mixing bowl using an electric mixer, cream the butter until it is fluffy, about 5 minutes. Add the confectioners' sugar about ½ cup at a time, beating on low speed after each addition until the sugar is well incorporated. When the sugar is fully incorporated, raise the mixer speed to medium-high and beat for about 2 minutes, until the mixture is fluffy. In a small mixing bowl, whisk together the vanilla and espresso powder. Add this mixture to the sugar and butter mixture, and beat to incorporate.

6. DECORATE AND SERVE THE CUPCAKES. Using a piping bag fitted with a plain or star-shaped tip, pipe the frosting onto the cupcakes in an outside-in spiral (see page 36). If you don't have a piping bag, use a resealable plastic bag with one of the corners snipped off, or simply spread the frosting onto the cupcakes with a knife. Top each cupcake with a chocolate-covered espresso bean (if using), and serve.

VANILLA CONFETTI CUPCAKES

Prep time: 20 MINUTES *Cook time:* 20 MINUTES *Makes:* 18 CUPCAKES

NUT-FREE

EQUIPMENT

2 standard 12-cup muffin tins, 18 paper cupcake liners, large mixing bowl, whisk, medium mixing bowl, rubber spatula, toothpick, electric mixer or stand mixer, piping bag and tip or resealable plastic bag (optional)

FOR THE CUPCAKES

½ cup (1 stick) unsalted butter, melted and cooled

1 cup granulated sugar

1 egg

¼ cup sour cream

¾ cup (whole or low-fat) milk

2 teaspoons vanilla extract

1⅔ cups all-purpose flour

½ teaspoon baking powder

¼ teaspoon baking soda

½ teaspoon salt

½ cup rainbow sprinkles, plus more for decorating

Bring on the rainbow sprinkles! These are the quintessential birthday cake cupcakes, but truthfully, they will make any old day a little brighter. Make them for your best friend, give them to your favorite teachers, or surprise your family with some of these colorful treats.

1. **PREHEAT THE OVEN AND PREPARE THE PANS.** Preheat the oven to 350°F. Put 18 paper liners in 2 muffin tins. It's okay that there will be 6 empty cups.

2. **COMBINE THE WET INGREDIENTS.** In a large mixing bowl, whisk together the melted butter and sugar. Add the egg, sour cream, milk, and vanilla and stir to mix well.

3. **COMBINE THE DRY INGREDIENTS.** In a medium mixing bowl, whisk together the flour, baking powder, baking soda, and salt. Add the dry mixture to the wet mixture, and stir until the batter is smooth. Using a rubber spatula, gently fold in the sprinkles.

4. **BAKE THE CUPCAKES.** Scoop the batter into the cupcake liners, filling each about two-thirds full. Bake in the preheated oven for 18 to 20 minutes, until a toothpick inserted into the center comes out clean. Remove the tins from the oven and set them on a wire rack to cool completely.

FOR THE FROSTING

¾ cup (1½ sticks) unsalted butter, at room temperature

3 cups confectioners' sugar

2 teaspoons vanilla extract

Pinch salt

2 to 4 tablespoons (whole or low-fat) milk

5. MAKE THE FROSTING. In the bowl of a stand mixer or in a large mixing bowl using an electric mixer, cream the butter on medium speed until it is creamy and smooth, about 3 minutes. Add the confectioners' sugar, vanilla, and salt, and beat on low until the sugar is incorporated into the butter. Add the milk a tablespoon at a time, beating to incorporate after each addition, just until the frosting reaches a good spreading or piping consistency, about 4 minutes more.

6. DECORATE AND SERVE THE CUPCAKES. Using a piping bag fitted with a plain or star-shaped tip, pipe the frosting onto the cupcakes in an outside-in spiral (see page 36). If you don't have a piping bag, you can use a resealable plastic bag with one of the corners snipped off, or simply spread the frosting onto the cupcakes with a knife. Top each cupcake with rainbow sprinkles and serve.

PINEAPPLE DUMP CAKE

WITH COCONUT FROSTING

Prep time: 10 MINUTES   *Cook time:* 40 MINUTES   *Serves:* 12

LEVEL **1**

NUT-FREE

EQUIPMENT
9-by-13-inch baking pan, large mixing bowl, saucepan, skewer or chopstick

FOR THE CAKE

Nonstick cooking spray

2 cups all-purpose flour

2 teaspoons baking soda

2 cups granulated sugar

2 eggs

½ teaspoon vanilla extract

2½ cups canned crushed pineapple, with juice

FOR THE FROSTING

½ cup (1 stick) unsalted butter

¾ cup evaporated milk

1 cup granulated sugar

1½ cups sweetened shredded coconut

A dump cake is pretty much what it sounds like—you dump the ingredients in a bowl, stir, and bake. It's the ultimate in easy baking. In fact, it's just as easy to make this from scratch as it is to make a cake from a boxed mix. While the cake bakes, cook the frosting on the stove top. You can have the whole thing done, from start to finish, in well under an hour. I love the flavors of coconut and pineapple together, which always makes me feel like I'm vacationing in the tropics.

1. **PREHEAT THE OVEN AND PREPARE THE PAN.** Preheat the oven to 350°F. Spray the baking pan with cooking spray.

2. **MIX THE CAKE BATTER.** In a large mixing bowl, stir together the flour, baking soda, sugar, eggs, vanilla, and crushed pineapple with its juice.

3. **BAKE THE CAKE.** Transfer the batter to the prepared baking pan, and bake in the preheated oven for 30 to 40 minutes, until the center of the cake is set.

4. **MAKE THE FROSTING.** While the cake is baking, in a saucepan over medium heat, combine the butter, evaporated milk, and sugar and cook, stirring frequently, until the mixture thickens, about 5 minutes. Stir in the coconut.

5. **FROST AND SERVE THE CAKE.** Remove the cake from the oven and immediately poke a dozen or so holes in it using a skewer or chopstick. Pour the hot frosting over the cake, and serve warm or at room temperature.

MUG CAKES IN THE MICROWAVE

Mug cakes—cakes that are mixed, baked, and served in heat-safe mugs—are a great solution when you're craving something sweet, but you don't want to bake a whole cake. You can mix them up quickly, and you're left with only one dish to clean. They take about 15 to 20 minutes to bake in the oven, but you know what makes them even better? The microwave! You can cook a mug cake in a microwave in only 1 to 2 minutes.

Whip together the Gingerbread Coffee Cake in a Mug (page 50) and pop it in the microwave for a quick breakfast—it will be your savior when you're in a rush.

To make a basic chocolate cake in a mug, take a large, microwave-safe mug and add 2 tablespoons of melted, unsalted butter, ¼ cup all-purpose flour, ¼ cup granulated sugar, 2 tablespoons unsweetened cocoa powder, ¼ teaspoon baking powder, ¼ cup milk, and ¼ teaspoon vanilla extract. Whisk until completely mixed. Stir in 2 tablespoons worth of chocolate chips if you want a fudgier cake. Microwave for 1½ to 2 minutes, until the cake is set. Then let it cool for a couple of minutes so you don't burn your tongue!

BLUEBERRY-SWIRL CHEESECAKE

Prep time: 20 MINUTES, PLUS 2 HOURS TO COOL AND OVERNIGHT TO CHILL
Cook time: 1 HOUR 25 MINUTES   *Serves:* 12 TO 14

LEVEL

NUT-FREE

EQUIPMENT

9-inch springform pan, medium mixing bowl, small saucepan, small bowl, medium bowl, fine-mesh sieve, large mixing bowl with electric mixer or stand mixer, aluminum foil, large baking dish or roasting pan, rubber spatula

FOR THE CRUST

Nonstick cooking spray

1½ cups graham cracker crumbs (about 12 whole graham crackers)

6 tablespoons unsalted butter, melted

¼ cup granulated sugar

FOR THE BLUEBERRY SWIRL

2 cups fresh or frozen blueberries

3 tablespoons granulated sugar

1 teaspoon freshly squeezed lemon juice

1 tablespoon cornstarch

1 tablespoon warm water

I love serving cheesecake in the summer—it's light and creamy, and I can take advantage of the seasonal blueberry harvest. The buttery graham cracker crust provides a satisfying crunchy base for the rich cheesecake layer, and the violet color of the sauce is absolutely beautiful. FYI, this one needs to chill overnight in the refrigerator before serving, so be sure to plan ahead.

1. **MAKE THE CRUST.** Preheat the oven to 350°F. Spray the springform pan with cooking spray. In a medium mixing bowl, stir the graham cracker crumbs with the butter and sugar until well combined. Press the mixture into the prepared pan, forming an even layer that covers the bottom of the pan and goes about ½ to 1 inch up the sides of the pan. Bake the crust in the preheated oven for 8 to 10 minutes, until it is lightly browned and firm. Remove the pan from the oven and set on a wire rack to cool.

2. **MAKE THE BLUEBERRY SWIRL.** In a small saucepan over medium heat, combine the blueberries and sugar and cook until the blueberries begin to break down and the sugar is completely dissolved, about 5 minutes. In a small bowl, stir together the lemon juice, cornstarch, and water, and add it to the blueberry mixture in the saucepan. Continue to cook, stirring, until the mixture begins to thicken, about 3 minutes more. Remove from the heat. Strain the sauce into a medium bowl through a fine-mesh sieve, reserving both the solids and the liquid separately.

FOR THE CHEESECAKE LAYER

3 (8-ounce) packages cream cheese, at room temperature

1 cup granulated sugar

1 cup sour cream

1½ teaspoons vanilla extract

3 eggs, at room temperature

Tip

No matter how careful you are, cheesecakes are prone to cracking on the top. To prevent this, make sure you start with room temperature ingredients, bake the cake in a water bath as directed, and let the cake cool slowly, first in the cooling oven and then at room temperature. If it cracks anyway, just cover it up with the blueberry sauce. It will still taste wonderful!

3. MAKE THE CHEESECAKE LAYER. In the bowl of a stand mixer or in a large mixing bowl using an electric mixer, beat the cream cheese on medium-high speed until smooth, 2 to 3 minutes. Add the sugar, and beat for about 3 minutes more, until the mixture is light and fluffy. Add the sour cream and vanilla extract, and beat just to combine. Add the eggs one at a time, beating after each addition until just incorporated.

4. ASSEMBLE THE CHEESECAKE. Wrap the bottom and sides of the springform pan with aluminum foil, and place in a large baking dish or roasting pan. Fill the baking dish with ½ to 1 inch of hot water. This is called a water bath. Pour the cream cheese mixture on top of the cooled crust, spreading it into an even layer with a rubber spatula. Drizzle about ¼ cup of the blueberry liquid on top of the cheesecake layer, and then use a knife to gently swirl it into the cheesecake in a decorative pattern. Combine the remaining blueberry juice with the reserved blueberry solids, and set aside for serving.

5. BAKE THE CHEESECAKE. Bake in the preheated oven for 55 to 65 minutes, until the top is mostly set but still jiggly in the center. Turn off the oven, crack the oven door open, and leave the cheesecake inside. Let cool in the oven for 1 hour. Remove the cheesecake from the oven and let cool completely. Cover and refrigerate overnight.

6. SERVE. Serve the cheesecake chilled and topped with the reserved berries and sauce.

CAMPFIRE S'MORES BAKED IN A GLASS

Prep time: 20 MINUTES   *Cook time:* 50 MINUTES   *Makes:* 8 CAKES

LEVEL 2

NUT-FREE

EQUIPMENT

6 6-ounce glass ramekins, medium mixing bowl, rimmed baking sheet, large mixing bowl with electric mixer or stand mixer, large mixing bowl, whisk, toothpick

FOR THE CRUST

Nonstick cooking spray

1¼ cups graham cracker crumbs (about 12 whole graham crackers)

6 tablespoons unsalted butter, melted

¼ cup granulated sugar

Pinch salt

(Ingredients continue on next page)

I'll bet you didn't know you could bake a cake in a glass. This take on a traditional campfire s'more is adorable and will look fabulous at a summer cookout. The graham cracker crust holds a rich chocolate cake, and toasted marshmallows are the crowning glory. I like to add chocolate chips to the cake batter to punch up the chocolate flavor, but it's also fine to leave them out.

1. **MAKE THE CRUST.** Preheat the oven to 350°F. Spray the insides of the glasses with cooking spray. In a medium mixing bowl, stir together the graham cracker crumbs, melted butter, sugar, and salt. Divide the mixture evenly among the prepared glasses, and press it into the bottoms with your thumbs or the back of a spoon to make an even layer covering the bottom and partway up the sides. Place the glasses on a rimmed baking sheet, and bake in the preheated oven for about 12 minutes, until the crusts puff up and turn golden brown.

2. **MAKE THE CAKE BATTER.** In the bowl of a stand mixer or in a large mixing bowl using an electric mixer, cream the butter and sugar together until light and fluffy, about 5 minutes. Add the eggs one at a time, beating to incorporate after each addition. Add the vanilla, and beat to mix. In a separate large mixing bowl, whisk together the flour, cocoa powder, baking powder, and salt. Add half of the dry mixture to the wet mixture, and beat just to incorporate. Add the cream, and beat to mix. Add the remaining dry mixture, and beat until just incorporated. Stir in the chocolate chips, if using. »

FOR THE CAKES

6 tablespoons unsalted butter, at room temperature

¾ cup granulated sugar

2 eggs

1 teaspoon vanilla extract

1 cup all-purpose flour

5 tablespoons unsweetened cocoa powder

1¼ teaspoons baking powder

½ teaspoon salt

6 tablespoons heavy (whipping) cream

¼ cup semisweet chocolate chips (optional)

FOR THE TOPPING

24 marshmallows

3. BAKE THE CAKES AND SERVE. Spoon the cake batter into the ramekins, dividing evenly. Bake in the preheated oven for about 30 minutes, until a toothpick inserted into the center comes out clean. Remove the baking sheet from the oven, and press 4 marshmallows down on top of each cake (be careful because the glass will be very hot!). Raise the oven temperature to 475°F, and return the baking sheet to the oven. Bake for 5 to 7 minutes more, until the marshmallows are soft and golden brown. Serve immediately. (Caution! Be sure to warn people that the ramekins are very hot.)

STRAWBERRY SHORTCAKE IN A JAR

Prep time: 20 MINUTES   *Cook time:* 15 MINUTES   *Makes:* 12 SERVINGS

LEVEL 2

NUT-FREE

EQUIPMENT
13-by-18-inch rimmed baking sheet, large mixing bowl with electric mixer or stand mixer, medium mixing bowl, whisk, rubber spatula, toothpick, 2 ½-inch round pastry or cookie cutter, 12 wide-mouth pint-size canning (or mason) jars

FOR THE SHORTCAKE

Nonstick cooking spray

⅓ cup unsalted butter, at room temperature

¾ cup granulated sugar

1 egg

2 teaspoons vanilla extract

1¾ cups all-purpose flour

2 teaspoons baking powder

¼ teaspoon salt

½ cup (whole or low-fat) milk

⅓ cup sour cream

2 cups sliced strawberries

Whipped cream, for topping

Strawberry shortcake is the official dessert of summer, but you can have it as soon as spring fever (and the first strawberry harvest) hits. Serving these cute cakes in mason jars looks beautiful on the dining room table. They can also be held in hand and eaten at more casual get-togethers like a cookout or a picnic.

1. **PREHEAT THE OVEN AND PREPARE THE PAN.** Preheat the oven to 350°F. Spray the baking sheet with cooking spray.

2. **MAKE THE SHORTCAKE BATTER.** In the bowl of a stand mixer or in a large mixing bowl using an electric mixer, cream the butter until is fluffy, about 2 minutes. Add the sugar, and beat to combine. Add the egg and vanilla, and beat to combine. In a medium mixing bowl, whisk together the flour, baking powder, and salt. Add half of the dry mixture to the butter mixture, and beat to combine. Add the milk, and beat to combine. Add the remaining dry mixture, and beat to combine. Beat in the sour cream.

3. **BAKE THE SHORTCAKE.** Pour the batter onto the prepared baking sheet, and use a rubber spatula to spread it into an even layer that covers the sheet completely. Bake in the preheated oven for 15 to 17 minutes, until a toothpick inserted into the center comes out clean. Remove from the oven and let cool on a wire rack.

4. **ASSEMBLE THE JARS.** Use the pastry cutter to cut out 24 rounds of shortcake. Put one shortcake round in the bottom of each jar. Top each with a layer of sliced strawberries. Put another shortcake round on top of the strawberry layer, followed by the remaining strawberries. Top each with whipped cream, and serve immediately.

6

PIES and TARTS

A well-baked pie is the stuff of legends, and everyone has a favorite—whether it's a classic apple pie or a billowing banana cream. Pies and tarts are similar in a lot of ways, but they have a few differences in terms of their makeup and reputation. Pies generally have a deeper crust (and often two crusts—one underneath the filling and one above) while tarts are simpler and sometimes seen as more refined. The key to success for both pies and tarts is the same, though: a flaky crust. Try your hand at a few of these recipes. Before you know it, you'll be a rock star at nailing that oh-so-delicious crust.

DEEP-DISH PEACH AND BLACKBERRY PIE

Prep time: 30 MINUTES, PLUS 10 MINUTES TO SIT, 1 HOUR TO CHILL THE DOUGH, AND 4 HOURS TO COOL

Cook time: 1 HOUR   *Serves:* 8

LEVEL

NUT-FREE

EQUIPMENT

Food processor or large bowl and pastry cutter (or two knives), plastic wrap, large mixing bowl, slotted spoon, rolling pin, 9-inch deep-dish pie plate, pastry brush, aluminum foil (if needed)

FOR THE CRUST

2½ cups all-purpose flour, plus more for rolling

2 tablespoons granulated sugar

½ teaspoon salt

1 cup plus 2 tablespoons cold, unsalted butter, cut into ½-inch pieces

4 to 7 tablespoons ice water or more, if needed

Peaches and blackberries are usually ripe at the same time in the summer, and that's great because they taste so good together. Buy your fruit from a farm stand or farmers' market if you can. Look for ripe, aromatic peaches and plump blackberries. Peeling, pitting, and slicing the peaches will take the most time in this recipe, but believe me, this pie is worth it! Serve the pie with a scoop of vanilla ice cream on top.

1. **MAKE THE CRUST.** In the bowl of a food processor or in a large mixing bowl, mix together the flour, sugar, and salt. Add the cold butter pieces and pulse, if using the food processor, or cut into the flour with a pastry cutter or two knives, until the mixture is in pea-size clumps. Add the ice water, 2 tablespoons at a time, and pulse or mix just until the dough comes together in a ball (you may not need to use all the water). Roll the dough into a ball, and flatten it into a disk shape. Wrap it tightly in plastic wrap and chill in the refrigerator for at least an hour.

2. **PREHEAT THE OVEN AND MAKE THE FILLING.** Preheat the oven to 450°F. In a large mixing bowl, stir together the peaches, brown sugar, ½ cup of granulated sugar, cinnamon, ginger, lemon juice, and cornstarch. Toss the blackberries with 1 tablespoon of the remaining sugar, and let the mixture sit for about 10 minutes. Using a slotted spoon, scoop the blackberries out of the bowl, leaving the juice behind, and add them to the peaches. If the mixture seems too dry, add a few spoonfuls of the blackberry juice.

FOR THE FILLING

3 pounds peaches, peeled, pitted, and sliced ½-inch thick

½ cup brown sugar

½ cup plus 3 tablespoons granulated sugar, divided

1 teaspoon ground cinnamon

½ teaspoon ground ginger

1 tablespoon freshly squeezed lemon juice

¼ cup cornstarch

1 cup fresh or frozen (thawed) blackberries

2 tablespoons cold butter, cut into small pieces

2 tablespoons (whole or low-fat) milk or cream

3. ROLL OUT THE DOUGH. Split the ball of dough into 2 equal pieces. On a lightly floured work surface, using a rolling pin, roll out each piece of dough into a circle about 14 inches across and ⅛ inch thick. Transfer one of the dough rounds to the pie plate by rolling it up onto the rolling pin and then unrolling it over the pie plate.

4. FILL THE PIE. Using a slotted spoon, lift the fruit out of the bowl and place it in the crust, leaving most of the juices behind. Dot the butter pieces over the fruit. Roll out the remaining dough into another 13- or 14-inch round, and place it on top of the pie. Trim the excess edges, leaving about a three-quarter-inch overhang. Fold under the edges of the dough, and crimp all the way around. With a sharp knife, cut several slits into the top crust to allow steam to escape. Using a pastry brush, brush the milk over the top crust, and sprinkle the remaining 2 tablespoons of sugar over the top.

5. BAKE THE PIE AND SERVE. Bake in the preheated oven for 10 minutes, then reduce the heat to 350°F and bake for 45 to 50 minutes more, or until the crust is golden brown and the juices are hot and bubbling. Check on the pie after 30 minutes or so. If the edges are already browning, wrap the edges in aluminum foil to keep them from burning. Remove from the oven and let cool for at least 4 hours before serving.

STRAWBERRY HAND PIES

Prep time: 30 MINUTES, PLUS 1 HOUR TO CHILL THE DOUGH   *Cook time:* 30 MINUTES   *Makes:* 8 PIES

EQUIPMENT

Food processor or large mixing bowl and pastry cutter (or two knives), plastic wrap, 2 large rimmed baking sheets, parchment paper, rolling pin, pastry brush, skewer or toothpick, small mixing bowl

FOR THE CRUST

2½ cups all-purpose flour, plus more for rolling

2 tablespoons granulated sugar

½ teaspoon salt

1 cup plus 2 tablespoons cold, unsalted butter, cut into ½-inch pieces

4 to 7 tablespoons ice water or more, if needed

FOR THE FILLING

¾ cup strawberry preserves

1 egg, lightly whisked

FOR THE GLAZE

¾ cup confectioners' sugar

2 to 3 tablespoons (whole or low-fat) milk

1 tablespoon strawberry preserves

These adorable handheld pies are the homemade version of a popular toaster pastry you can buy in supermarkets. They're simple to make, and they taste a million times better than the packaged version. Your parents will approve of these, since they don't contain any weird ingredients like preservatives or high-fructose corn syrup.

1. MAKE THE DOUGH. In the bowl of a food processor or in a large mixing bowl, mix together the flour, sugar, and salt. Add the cold butter pieces and pulse, if using the food processor, or cut into the flour with a pastry cutter or two knives, until the mixture is in pea-size clumps. Add the ice water, 2 tablespoons at a time, and pulse or mix just until the dough comes together in a ball (you may not need to use all the water). Roll the dough into a ball, and flatten it into a disk shape. Wrap it tightly in plastic wrap and chill in the refrigerator for at least an hour.

2. PREHEAT THE OVEN AND PREPARE THE PANS. Preheat the oven to 375°F. Line the baking sheets with parchment paper.

3. ROLL OUT THE DOUGH. Split the dough into two equal pieces. On a lightly floured work surface, use a rolling pin to roll out each piece of dough to a 13-by-11-inch rectangle about ⅛ inch thick. Trim the edges so the sides are straight, and cut each sheet into eight 5-by-3-inch rectangles.

4. ASSEMBLE THE PIES. Arrange 8 rectangles on the prepared baking sheets, leaving at least an inch of space between them. Dollop about 1½ tablespoons of the preserves onto each rectangle, spreading it down the center but leaving a clear border of at least half an inch. Brush the edges of the dough with the whisked egg. Place the remaining 8 rectangles of dough on top of the preserves, and seal the edges together. Press the tines of a fork into the border of the dough to make a decorative edge all the way around each rectangle. With a skewer or toothpick, prick several holes in the top of each pie. This will allow steam to release from the hand pies as they bake. »

5. BAKE THE PIES. Place both baking sheets in the preheated oven together, and bake for 15 minutes. Rotate the pans (switching from top to bottom and rotating them back to front), then continue to bake for 10 to 15 minutes more, until the crusts are golden brown and the filling is bubbling out of the holes. Transfer the pies to a wire rack to cool.

6. MAKE THE GLAZE, DRIZZLE, AND SERVE. In a small mixing bowl, stir together the confectioners' sugar, 2 tablespoons of milk, and the preserves until smooth. Add additional milk as needed for a pourable consistency. Drizzle the glaze over the tops of the pies while they are still warm. Let the pies cool and the glaze dry. Serve at room temperature.

Tip

To make these ahead of time, assemble the pies and freeze them on the baking sheets before baking. Once frozen, transfer them to resealable plastic bags and store in the freezer for up to 3 months. Bake the pies straight from the freezer as directed, adding a few minutes to the cooking time. Make the glaze and top the pies after baking.

THE LONG AND THE SHORT ABOUT SHORTCUTS

Is it okay to take shortcuts when baking? The short answer is yes!

Let me explain. A pie crust made from scratch is always better than a store-bought crust, but we all get busy sometimes, so if it saves you time, go ahead and buy a prepared crust. If you're doing this, look for ones that are made with real butter—not shortening—for the best flavor and quality.

I confess, I buy prepared crusts myself, sometimes. Taking shortcuts like this is not a bad thing, as long as you substitute the highest-quality store-bought items you can find. But before you head to the store, make sure the shortcut is really necessary. The recipes in this book tell you how long it takes to prepare and bake each recipe. If you want to make brownies, you'll find that you can make them just as quickly from scratch as you would if you bought a boxed mix. The difference is that the boxed mix is full of preservatives and other processed ingredients that keep the boxed mix "shelf stable" for a long time—usually for years. Why consume all that nonsense if you don't have to? If you make brownies yourself, you'll have the pleasure of knowing exactly what ingredients went into them.

Store-bought shortcuts that are worth buying include things like frozen puff pastry, crushed graham crackers, and phyllo dough. These items will save you time without any loss of quality or flavor.

APPLE PIE

WITH CINNAMON-STREUSEL TOPPING

Prep time: 30 MINUTES, PLUS 1 HOUR TO CHILL THE DOUGH AND 4 HOURS TO COOL

Cook time: 50 MINUTES   *Serves:* 8

LEVEL 2

NUT-FREE

EQUIPMENT

Food processor or large mixing bowl with pastry cutter (or two knives), plastic wrap, rolling pin, 9-inch deep-dish pie plate, large mixing bowl, small mixing bowl, whisk, pastry brush, aluminum foil (if needed)

FOR THE CRUST

1¼ cups all-purpose flour, plus more for rolling

1 tablespoon granulated sugar

¼ teaspoon salt

½ cup (1 stick) plus 1 tablespoon cold, unsalted butter, cut into ½-inch pieces

2 to 4 tablespoons ice water or more, if needed

1 egg, lightly beaten, for brushing

Apple pie is a classic, and this one is especially impressive with its crunchy and flavorful topping. My family requests this pie every Thanksgiving. It is great on its own, but I can't resist serving it with a scoop of vanilla ice cream. I like to use crisp and tart-sweet Granny Smith apples here.

1. MAKE THE CRUST. In the bowl of a food processor or in a large mixing bowl, mix together the flour, sugar, and salt. Add the cold butter pieces and pulse, if using the food processor, or cut into the flour with a pastry cutter or two knives until the mixture is in pea-size clumps. Add the ice water 2 tablespoons at a time and pulse or mix, adding additional ice water as needed, just until the dough comes together in a ball (you may not need to use all the water). Roll the dough into a ball, and flatten it into a disk shape. Wrap it tightly in plastic wrap and chill in the refrigerator for at least an hour.

2. PREHEAT THE OVEN AND ROLL OUT THE DOUGH. First, preheat the oven to 450°F. On a lightly floured work surface, use a rolling pin to roll out the dough into a circle about 14 inches across and ⅛ inch thick. Transfer the dough round to the pie plate by rolling it up onto the rolling pin and then unrolling it over the pie dish. Trim any excess dough from the edges, leaving about a ¾-inch overhang.

3. MAKE THE FILLING. In a large mixing bowl, toss the apple slices with the lemon juice. In a small mixing bowl, whisk together the brown sugar, salt, cornstarch, and cinnamon. Sprinkle the mixture over the apples, and toss gently to coat the apples.

FOR THE FILLING

5 to 6 cups apples, peeled, cored, and thinly sliced

2 tablespoons freshly squeezed lemon juice

½ cup brown sugar

⅛ teaspoon salt

1 tablespoon cornstarch

½ teaspoon ground cinnamon

FOR THE TOPPING

¾ cup all-purpose flour

¾ cup rolled oats

½ cup brown sugar

½ teaspoon ground cinnamon

½ cup cold, unsalted butter, cut into small pieces

4. ASSEMBLE THE PIE AND BAKE. Transfer the apples to the pie crust, spreading them out so they completely cover the bottom. Crimp the edges of the crust, and brush them with the egg. Bake in the preheated oven for 10 minutes.

5. MAKE THE TOPPING. While the pie is in the oven, in a medium mixing bowl or the bowl of a food processor, combine the flour, oats, brown sugar, and cinnamon. Pulse or use a pastry cutter or two knives to cut in the butter until the mixture resembles a coarse meal.

6. FINISH THE PIE AND SERVE. Remove the pie from the oven, and reduce the oven temperature to 375°F. Sprinkle the streusel topping over the top of the pie in an even layer. Return the pie to the oven, and continue to bake for 35 to 40 minutes more, until the topping is golden brown and the filling is bubbling. If the topping is browning too quickly, cover it with aluminum foil. Remove from the oven and let cool for at least 4 hours before serving.

BANANA CREAM PIE

Prep time: 30 MINUTES, PLUS SEVERAL HOURS OR OVERNIGHT TO CHILL   *Cook time:* 15 MINUTES   *Serves:* 8

LEVEL

NUT-FREE

EQUIPMENT
Medium saucepan, 9-inch pie plate, medium mixing bowl

FOR THE FILLING

2 cups (whole or low-fat) milk

⅔ cup sugar

3 tablespoons cornstarch

Pinch salt

1 egg plus 1 egg yolk

2 tablespoons unsalted butter

2 teaspoons vanilla extract

2 large bananas, sliced

2 cups whipped cream

½ cup caramel sauce (optional)

FOR THE CRUST

Nonstick cooking spray

1½ cups graham cracker crumbs (about 12 whole graham crackers)

6 tablespoons unsalted butter, melted

¼ cup granulated sugar

A graham cracker crust filled with fresh bananas and a silky vanilla custard make this pie delightful. The drizzle of caramel sauce is optional, but it really amps up the deliciousness factor. Pro-tip: Keep an eye on the custard while it's cooking. It can go from thick to boiling over and scorched in a matter of seconds.

1. **MAKE THE FILLING.** In a medium saucepan over medium heat, stir together the milk, sugar, cornstarch, salt, egg, and egg yolk. Heat, stirring frequently, until the mixture bubbles and thickens, about 4 minutes. Remove the pan from the heat, and stir in the butter and vanilla. Let cool for about 15 minutes. Cover and refrigerate for at least 30 minutes.

2. **MAKE AND BAKE THE CRUST.** Preheat the oven to 350°F. Spray the pie plate with cooking spray. In a medium mixing bowl, stir the graham cracker crumbs with the butter and sugar until well combined. Press the mixture into the prepared pie plate, forming an even layer that covers the bottom and sides of the plate. Bake the crust in the preheated oven for 8 to 10 minutes until lightly browned and firm. Remove the pie plate from the oven and set on a wire rack to cool.

3. **ASSEMBLE THE PIE.** Pour half of the filling mixture into the crust, spreading it into an even layer. Top with the banana slices. Pour the remaining filling mixture over the bananas and smooth into an even layer. Cover and chill in the refrigerator for several hours or overnight.

4. **FINISH AND SERVE THE PIE.** Just before serving, spread the whipped cream in an even layer over the top of the pie. Drizzle the caramel sauce over the top (if using), and serve immediately.

If you prefer, you can use a nondairy whipped topping like Cool Whip in place of the whipped cream.

CHOCOLATE-PEANUT BUTTER CUP PIE

Prep time: 15 MINUTES, PLUS 30 MINUTES TO CHILL   *Cook time:* 10 MINUTES   *Serves:* 8

LEVEL

EQUIPMENT

2 medium mixing bowls, 9-inch pie plate, large mixing bowl with electric mixer or stand mixer, rubber spatula, medium microwave-safe bowl or pitcher, whisk

FOR THE CRUST

25 chocolate sandwich cookies (like Oreos), crushed into fine crumbs

¼ cup unsalted butter, melted

FOR THE FILLING

½ cup (1 stick) unsalted butter, at room temperature

1½ cups smooth peanut butter

1 cup confectioners' sugar

FOR THE TOPPING

¾ cup heavy (whipping) cream

6 ounces semisweet chocolate, chopped

A chocolate cookie crumb crust holds a dreamy peanut butter filling topped with a rich chocolate ganache. I have to be careful when I make this pie because I cannot stop eating it. Fortunately, everyone else seems to love it as much as I do and it always disappears quickly at a party or family gathering (and not just into my own belly!).

1. MAKE THE CRUST. Preheat the oven to 350°F. In a medium mixing bowl, stir to combine the cookie crumbs and melted butter. Press the mixture into the pie plate, using your hands or the bottom of a glass to press it into an even layer covering the bottom and sides of the pan. Bake in the preheated oven for 8 to 10 minutes. Remove from the oven and set on a wire rack to cool completely.

2. MAKE THE FILLING. In the bowl of a stand mixer or in a large mixing bowl using an electric mixer, beat together the butter, peanut butter, and confectioners' sugar until creamy. Spoon the mixture into the cooled crust, smoothing the top with a rubber spatula. Cover and place the filled crust in the freezer.

3. MAKE THE TOPPING. Pour the cream into a medium microwave-safe bowl or pitcher, and heat in the microwave for 1 minute. Put the chocolate into a medium mixing bowl, and pour the hot cream over the top. Let the mixture sit for a few minutes until the chocolate begins to melt. Whisk until the chocolate is completely melted and the mixture is smooth. Let cool for about 5 minutes.

4. TOP THE PIE AND SERVE. Pour the chocolate topping over the pie, spreading it into a smooth layer with a rubber spatula. Return the pie to the freezer and freeze until set, 20 to 30 minutes. Serve chilled.

KIWI AND STRAWBERRY TART

WITH VANILLA PASTRY CREAM

Prep time: 30 MINUTES, PLUS 3 HOURS TO CHILL THE FILLING   *Cook time:* 20 MINUTES   *Serves:* 8

LEVEL 3

NUT-FREE

EQUIPMENT

Medium saucepan, medium mixing bowl, whisk, ladle or measuring cup, plastic wrap, food processor or large mixing bowl and pastry cutter (or two knives), rolling pin, 9-inch round tart pan with a removable bottom, parchment paper, pie weights or dried beans, small microwave-safe bowl, pastry brush, platter

---

FOR THE FILLING

2 cups whole milk

½ cup granulated sugar, divided

Pinch salt

5 egg yolks

3 tablespoons cornstarch

¼ cup cold, unsalted butter, cut into 4 pieces

1 teaspoon vanilla extract

Pastry cream is something special. It's a thick custard used for pie and tart fillings, and every serious baker should know how to make it. Combine it with fresh fruit, and you've got yourself a treat! If you can't find ripe kiwis or strawberries, you can substitute just about any fruit when you're making this tart—berries, pears, peaches, nectarines, mangos, or even bananas will all be great.

1. **MAKE THE PASTRY CREAM.** In a medium saucepan set over medium heat, combine the milk, ¼ cup plus 2 tablespoons of sugar, and the salt and heat, stirring occasionally, until the milk simmers and the sugar is dissolved, about 5 minutes.

2. **WHISK THE EGG YOLKS.** While the milk is heating, in a medium mixing bowl, whisk the egg yolks. Add the remaining 2 tablespoons of sugar, and whisk until the mixture is light and creamy, about 5 minutes. Whisk in the cornstarch.

3. **TEMPER THE EGG YOLKS.** When the milk comes to a simmer, pour about ½ cup of it into a ladle or measuring cup and, while whisking continuously, add it slowly to the yolks. Add the entire yolk mixture to the hot milk in the saucepan, and continue to heat, whisking constantly, until the mixture thickens and becomes glossy, about 3 minutes more. Stir in the vanilla. Transfer to a medium bowl and cover with plastic wrap, pressing the plastic directly onto the surface of the cream to keep a skin from forming. Chill in the refrigerator for at least 3 hours.

FOR THE CRUST

1⅓ cups all-purpose flour

½ teaspoon salt

½ cup (1 stick) cold, unsalted butter, cut into small pieces

¼ cup ice water

½ teaspoon vinegar

FOR THE TOPPING

4 kiwi, peeled and cut into rounds

1 cup halved fresh strawberries

2 tablespoons strawberry jam

4. MAKE THE CRUST. In the bowl of a food processor or in a large mixing bowl, combine the flour and salt. Add the butter and, using the food processor, pastry cutter, or two knives, cut the butter into the flour until the mixture forms pea-size lumps. Slowly add the ice water, pulsing the food processor or mixing by hand, until the dough begins to hold together. Add the vinegar, and mix until the dough forms a ball. Flatten the ball into a disk shape, wrap it tightly in plastic wrap, and refrigerate for at least 30 minutes.

5. PREHEAT THE OVEN AND ROLL OUT THE DOUGH. Preheat the oven to 400°F. On a lightly floured work surface, use a rolling pin to roll out the dough into a circle about 11 inches across and ⅛ inch thick. Transfer the dough round to the tart pan by rolling it up onto the rolling pin and then unrolling it over the tart pan. Press the dough into the bottom and sides. Trim off any excess.

6. BLIND BAKE THE CRUST. Line the dough with parchment paper, and fill it with pie weights or dried beans. Bake in the preheated oven for 10 minutes. Lift out the pie weights and parchment, and cook the crust for another 6 to 8 minutes, until golden brown. Remove from the oven and let cool completely on a wire rack.

7. FILL AND DECORATE THE TART. Just before serving, fill the tart shell with the pastry cream. Arrange the fruit on top in a decorative manner (try alternating concentric circles [a large circle on the outside with gradually smaller circles within] with the kiwi slices partially overlapping). In a small, microwave-safe bowl, heat the jam in the microwave for 15 to 20 seconds, then brush it over the fruit. Carefully lift the tart out of the outer ring of the tart pan (keep the metal bottom of the pan in place), and place it on a platter to serve.

LEMON CHESS PIE

Prep time: 20 MINUTES, PLUS 1 HOUR TO CHILL   *Cook time:* 50 MINUTES   *Serves:* 8

LEVEL

NUT-FREE

EQUIPMENT

Large mixing bowl and pastry cutter or food processor, plastic wrap, rolling pin, 9-inch deep-dish pie plate, large mixing bowl, whisk, pastry brush

FOR THE CRUST

1¼ cups all-purpose flour, plus more for rolling

1 tablespoon granulated sugar

¼ teaspoon salt

½ cup (1 stick) plus 1 tablespoon cold, unsalted butter, cut into ½-inch pieces

2 to 4 tablespoons ice water or more, if needed

1 egg, lightly beaten, for brushing

FOR THE FILLING

6 tablespoons butter, melted

1⅔ cups sugar

5 eggs, lightly beaten

¾ cup freshly squeezed lemon juice

1½ tablespoons cornstarch

1 tablespoon cornmeal

½ teaspoon salt

This simple pie has the zing of a lemon meringue pie, but it's much easier to make. The secret is that the rich custard filling is flavored with lots of fresh lemon juice, and the top browns as it bakes, giving it a deep, caramel-like flavor. Those two flavors fuse into something magical.

1. MAKE THE CRUST. In the bowl of a food processor or in a large mixing bowl, mix together the flour, sugar, and salt. Add the cold butter pieces and pulse, if using the food processor, or cut into the flour with a pastry cutter or two knives, until the mixture is in pea-size clumps. Add the ice water 2 tablespoons at a time, and pulse or mix, adding additional ice water as needed, just until the dough comes together in a ball (you may not need to use all the water). Roll the dough into a ball, then flatten it into a disk shape. Wrap it tightly in plastic wrap and chill in the refrigerator for at least an hour.

2. PREHEAT THE OVEN AND ROLL OUT THE DOUGH. First, preheat the oven to 375°F. On a lightly floured work surface, use a rolling pin to roll the dough out into a circle about 14 inches across and about ⅛ inch thick. Transfer the dough round to the pie plate by rolling it up onto the rolling pin and then unrolling it over the pie plate. Trim any excess dough from the edges, leaving about a ¾-inch overhang. Refrigerate.

3. MAKE THE FILLING. In a large mixing bowl, whisk together the butter and sugar. Add the eggs, lemon juice, cornstarch, cornmeal, and salt, and mix to combine well. Pour the filling into the chilled crust. Brush the crust with the beaten egg.

4. BAKE AND SERVE THE PIE. Bake in the preheated oven for 45 to 50 minutes, until the top of the filling and the crust are golden brown. Remove from the oven, and let cool for at least 1 hour before serving.

PISTACHIO-BLACKBERRY TART

Prep time: 30 MINUTES PLUS 30 MINUTES TO CHILL DOUGH   *Cook time:* 1 HOUR   *Serves:* 8

LEVEL

EQUIPMENT

Food processor, plastic wrap, rolling pin, parchment paper, 9-inch tart pan with a removable bottom, pie weights or dried beans, small microwave-safe bowl

FOR THE CRUST

1⅓ cups all-purpose flour

½ teaspoon salt

½ cup (1 stick) cold, unsalted butter, cut into small pieces

¼ cup ice water

½ teaspoon vinegar

FOR THE FILLING

½ cup plus 2 tablespoons shelled unsalted pistachios

¼ cup plus 1 tablespoon granulated sugar

2 teaspoons grated orange zest

⅛ teaspoon baking powder

3 tablespoons unsalted butter, at room temperature

1 egg

2 cups fresh blackberries

2 tablespoons orange marmalade

This tart is so pretty with its bright greens and purples. If you don't have blackberries, though, it will still look gorgeous and taste incredible with strawberries or raspberries. The uniquely delightful filling is made by grinding pistachios with sugar to make a paste that's similar to marzipan, an almond paste used frequently in pies, tarts, and cakes found in bakeries.

1. **MAKE THE DOUGH.** In the bowl of a food processor, combine the flour and salt. Add the butter, and process to cut the butter into the flour until the mixture forms pea-size lumps. Slowly add the ice water, pulsing the food processor, until the dough begins to hold together. Add the vinegar, and mix until the dough forms a ball. Flatten the ball into a disk shape, wrap it tightly in plastic wrap, and refrigerate for at least 30 minutes.

2. **PREHEAT THE OVEN AND ROLL OUT THE CRUST.** Preheat the oven to 400°F. On a lightly floured work surface, use a rolling pin to roll out the dough into a circle about 11 inches across and ⅛ inch thick. Transfer the dough round to the tart pan by rolling it up onto the rolling pin and then unrolling it over the tart pan. Press the dough into the bottom and sides. Trim off any excess.

3. **MAKE THE FILLING.** In the bowl of the food processor, combine ½ cup of pistachios and ¼ cup of granulated sugar with the orange zest and baking powder, and pulse to finely grind the nuts. Add the butter and egg, and pulse to blend.

4. **BLIND BAKE THE CRUST.** Line the dough with parchment paper and fill it with pie weights or dried beans. Bake in the preheated oven for 10 minutes. Lift out the pie weights and parchment and let cool completely on a wire rack. »

5. FILL, TOP, AND BAKE. Spread the filling mixture evenly over the bottom of the cooled crust. Toss the blackberries with the remaining 1 tablespoon of sugar, and then spoon them over the top of the filling, arranging them in a single layer. Bake in the preheated oven for 50 to 60 minutes, until the filling is puffed and golden. Remove from the oven and let cool to room temperature.

6. FINISH AND SERVE. In a small, microwavable bowl, heat the marmalade in the microwave for about 20 seconds. Brush it all over the blackberries. Finely chop the remaining 2 tablespoons of pistachios, and sprinkle them over the top. Cut into wedges to serve.

UPSIDE-DOWN CARAMEL-APPLE TART
(TARTE TATIN)

Prep time: 20 MINUTES, PLUS 10 MINUTES TO COOL   *Cook time:* 50 MINUTES   *Serves:* 8

LEVEL

NUT-FREE

EQUIPMENT

Large mixing bowl, rolling pin, 10-inch plate or skillet, baking sheet, medium skillet, whisk, 9-inch round cake pan, platter

3 to 4 pounds apples (Granny Smith, Fuji, Honeycrisp), peeled, cored, and each cut into 4 wedges

2 tablespoons freshly squeezed lemon juice

1¼ cups granulated sugar, divided

1 sheet frozen puff pastry, thawed according to package directions

6 tablespoons unsalted butter, at room temperature

A *tarte tatin* is quite elegant and yet so simple to prepare. Bake this when you want to impress someone. It uses only 5 ingredients, including a store-bought puff pastry sheet you can find in the freezer section of any supermarket. Look for one that uses butter instead of vegetable shortening for the best flavor. Thaw the pastry according to the directions on the package.

1. **PREPARE THE APPLES.** In a large mixing bowl, toss the apple wedges with the lemon juice and ¼ cup of the sugar. Let stand for 15 minutes.

2. **PREPARE THE PASTRY.** Use a rolling pin on a lightly floured work surface to roll out the pastry sheet to a square about 10½-by-10½ inches. Using a 10-inch plate or skillet as a guide, cut the dough into a 10-inch circle. Place the pastry on a baking sheet and refrigerate.

3. **PREHEAT THE OVEN TO 425°F.**

4. **MAKE THE CARAMEL.** In a medium skillet over medium-high heat, melt the butter. Sprinkle the remaining 1 cup of sugar over the butter in an even layer. Cook, whisking constantly, until the sugar is fully dissolved and the mixture turns golden, about 10 minutes.

5. **FORM THE TART.** Pour the caramel mixture into the cake pan. Drain the apples, and arrange them in a nice pattern on top of the caramel with the cut sides up. »

6. BAKE IN THE OVEN. Bake the apples and caramel in the preheated oven for about 20 minutes.

7. ADD THE PASTRY. Remove the pan from the oven, and lay the pastry round on top of the apples, fitting it into the pan. Return to the oven and bake for about 20 minutes more, until the crust is nicely browned. Remove the pan from the oven and place it on a wire rack to cool for 10 minutes.

8. UNMOLD THE TART AND SERVE. Just before serving, run a knife around the edge of the pan to loosen the caramel. Lay a platter upside-down on top of the tart and, using sturdy potholders, carefully turn the whole thing over so that the tart drops out of the pan onto the platter. If any of the apples stick to the pan, just pull them off and place them on top of the tart. Drizzle any leftover caramel over the top. Serve warm.

KEY LIME TART

Prep time: 30 MINUTES, PLUS 1 HOUR TO COOL AND 2 HOURS TO CHILL   *Cook time:* 40 MINUTES   *Serves:* 8

LEVEL

NUT-FREE

EQUIPMENT

Food processor or large mixing bowl and pastry cutter (or two knives), plastic wrap, rolling pin, 9-inch tart pan with a removable bottom, parchment paper, pie weights or dried beans, medium mixing bowl

FOR THE CRUST

1⅓ cups all-purpose flour

½ teaspoon salt

½ cup (1 stick) cold, unsalted butter, cut into small pieces

¼ cup ice water

½ teaspoon vinegar

FOR THE FILLING

1 (14-ounce) can sweetened condensed milk

4 egg yolks

2 teaspoons Key lime zest

¾ cup Key lime juice (about 15 Key limes)

Key limes (also called Mexican limes) are named for the Florida Keys. They are smaller, more tart, and more aromatic than the more common Persian limes you find in most supermarkets. Because they are small, you need quite a few of them to get the quantity of juice needed for this tart, but it's well worth it. If you can't find Key limes, look for Key lime juice sold in a bottle. You'll find it alongside the bottles of lemon juice in the supermarket. You can also substitute juice from "regular" limes if absolutely necessary—the tart won't have that distinctive Key lime flavor, but it will still be delicious!

1. **MAKE THE CRUST.** In the bowl of a food processor or a large mixing bowl, combine the flour and salt. Add the butter and, using the food processor, pastry cutter, two knives, or the food processor, cut the butter into the flour until the mixture forms pea-size lumps. Slowly add the ice water, pulsing the food processor or mixing by hand, until the dough begins to hold together. Add the vinegar, and mix until the dough forms a ball. Flatten the ball into a disk shape, wrap it tightly in plastic wrap, and refrigerate for at least 30 minutes.

2. **PREHEAT THE OVEN AND ROLL OUT THE DOUGH.** Preheat the oven to 400°F. On a lightly floured work surface, use a rolling pin to roll out the dough into a circle about 11 inches across and ⅛ inch thick. Transfer the dough round to the tart pan by rolling it up onto the rolling pin and then unrolling it over the tart pan. Press the dough into the bottom and sides. Trim off any excess. »

3. BLIND BAKE THE DOUGH. Line the dough with parchment paper, and fill it with pie weights or dried beans. Bake in the pre-heated oven for 10 minutes. Remove from the oven, lift out the pie weights and parchment, and let cool completely on a wire rack. Reduce the oven temperature to 350°F.

4. MAKE THE FILLING. In a medium mixing bowl, stir together the sweetened condensed milk, egg yolks, lime zest, and lime juice until well combined and smooth. Pour the filling into the cooled tart shell, and bake in the preheated oven for about 30 minutes, until the crust is golden brown and the filling is mostly set.

5. COOL, CHILL, AND SERVE THE TART. Set the tart on a wire rack to cool to room temperature, then chill it in the refrigerator for at least 2 hours. Serve chilled.

CHOCOLATE-CHERRY BLACK FOREST TART

Prep time: 30 MINUTES, PLUS 1 HOUR TO COOL AND 3 HOURS TO CHILL
Cook time: 1 HOUR 5 MINUTES   *Serves:* 8

LEVEL 3

NUT-FREE

EQUIPMENT

Small mixing bowl, whisk, food processor or large mixing bowl with whisk and pastry cutter (or two knives), plastic wrap, rolling pin, 9-inch tart pan with a removable bottom, parchment paper, pie weights or dried beans, medium microwave-safe bowl, large bowl with electric mixer or stand mixer

FOR THE CRUST

1 egg yolk

1 tablespoon heavy (whipping) cream

½ teaspoon vanilla extract

1 cup all-purpose flour

¼ cup unsweetened cocoa powder

⅔ cup confectioners' sugar

¼ teaspoon salt

½ cup (1 stick) cold, unsalted butter, cut into small pieces

(Ingredients continue on next page)

If you are a hardcore chocolate-lover, prepare to be wowed. The crust in this recipe is enriched with cocoa powder and then packed with a creamy chocolate filling studded with pitted fresh cherries. A topping of sweetened whipped cream, more cherries, and shavings of semisweet chocolate finish it off.

1. MAKE THE CRUST. In a small mixing bowl, whisk together the egg yolk, cream, and vanilla. In the bowl of a food processor or in a large mixing bowl, combine the flour, cocoa powder, sugar, and salt and pulse or whisk to mix. Add the butter and, using the food processor, pastry cutter, or two knives, cut the butter into the flour until the mixture forms pea-size lumps. Add the egg yolk mixture and pulse or mix just until the dough comes together. Form the dough into a disk shape, and wrap it tightly in plastic wrap. Chill in the refrigerator for at least 1 hour.

2. PREHEAT THE OVEN AND ROLL OUT AND BLIND BAKE THE CRUST. Preheat the oven to 375°F. Use a rolling pin to roll the dough out on a lightly floured work surface into a circle about 12 inches across. Transfer the dough round to the tart pan by rolling it up onto the rolling pin and then unrolling it over the tart pan. Press the dough into the bottom and sides. Trim off any excess. Line the dough with parchment paper, and fill it with pie weights or dried beans. Bake in the preheated oven for 30 minutes. Remove the parchment lining and weights, then return the crust to the oven and bake for 6 to 8 minutes more, until the crust is golden brown. Place on a wire rack to cool completely. Leave the oven on. »

FOR THE FILLING

6 ounces semisweet or bittersweet chocolate, chopped

6 tablespoons unsalted butter, cut into pieces

¾ cup brown sugar

3 eggs

½ teaspoon salt

1 teaspoon vanilla extract

2 cups pitted cherries, divided

1 cup heavy (whipping) cream

2 tablespoons confectioners' sugar

Semisweet chocolate, shaved, for decorating

3. MAKE THE FILLING. In a medium microwave-safe bowl, heat the chocolate and butter on 50 percent power for 1 minute. Stir the mixture. If the chocolate isn't fully melted, heat on 50 percent power in 30-second intervals, stirring in between, until the chocolate is melted and the mixture is smooth. In the bowl of a stand mixer or in a large mixing bowl using an electric mixer, beat the brown sugar, eggs, salt, and vanilla together on high speed for about 2 minutes until light and fluffy. With the mixer running, slowly add the melted chocolate mixture to the egg mixture. Beat until well combined.

4. BAKE THE TART. Pour the filling into the cooled crust, and top with 1 cup of pitted cherries. Bake for 25 minutes, then set on a wire rack to cool for 30 minutes. Refrigerate and chill for at least 2 hours.

5. ASSEMBLE AND SERVE THE TART. In a large mixing bowl, beat the cream and confectioners' sugar until the mixture holds soft peaks (see page 31). Spread the whipped cream over the filling. Top with the remaining 1 cup of pitted cherries and chocolate shavings. Serve immediately or refrigerate until ready to serve.

CHOCOLATE-HAZELNUT TART

Prep time: 30 MINUTES, PLUS 1 HOUR TO CHILL CRUST AND 30 MINUTES TO COOL

Cook time: 1 HOUR 20 MINUTES   *Serves:* 8

LEVEL

EQUIPMENT

Food processor, plastic wrap, rolling pin, 9-inch tart pan with a removable bottom, parchment paper, pie weights or dried beans, large mixing bowl, rubber spatula

FOR THE CRUST

½ cup hazelnuts, toasted (see tip)

½ cup confectioners' sugar

1 cup all-purpose flour

⅛ teaspoon salt

5 tablespoons cold, unsalted butter, cut into ¼-inch pieces and chilled

1 egg

½ teaspoon vanilla extract

If you love the rich, nutty, chocolatey flavor of a certain chocolate-hazelnut spread that comes in a jar, you need to bake this tart. Ground hazelnuts give the crust extra flavor and crunch, too. This is also an impressive dessert to end a holiday meal.

1. **MAKE THE CRUST.** In the bowl of a food processor, combine the hazelnuts and sugar and process until the nuts are finely ground. Add the flour and salt, and pulse to mix. Add the butter and pulse several times, until the mixture resembles a coarse meal. With the processor running, add the egg and vanilla through the tube in the top. Process until the dough just comes together in a ball. Remove the dough from the food processor, flatten it into a disk, and wrap it tightly in plastic wrap. Refrigerate for at least 1 hour.

2. **PREHEAT THE OVEN AND ROLL OUT AND BLIND BAKE THE CRUST.** Preheat the oven to 375°F. On a lightly floured work surface, use a rolling pin to roll out the dough to a circle about 11 inches across. Transfer the dough round to the tart pan by rolling it up onto the rolling pin and then unrolling it over the tart pan. Press the dough into the bottom and sides. Trim off any excess. Line the crust with parchment paper, and fill it with pie weights or dried beans. Bake in the preheated oven for 20 minutes. Place the pan on a wire rack and let cool. Reduce the oven heat to 325°F.

FOR THE FILLING

½ cup sugar

2 tablespoons
all-purpose flour

3 eggs, lightly beaten

1½ cups hazelnuts, peeled,
chopped, and toasted

1 cup semisweet
chocolate chips

¾ cup corn syrup

2 tablespoons butter, melted

1 teaspoon vanilla extract

¼ teaspoon salt

3. MAKE THE FILLING. In a large mixing bowl, stir together the sugar and flour. Add the eggs, nuts, chocolate chips, corn syrup, melted butter, vanilla, and salt, and stir to mix well. Spoon the filling into the prepared crust, smoothing into an even layer with a rubber spatula.

4. BAKE THE TART AND SERVE. Bake in the preheated oven for 1 hour. Remove from the oven and place on a wire rack to cool for at least 30 minutes before serving.

Hazelnuts have a papery peel on them that can be bitter. To remove the peel and toast hazelnuts: Spread the nuts in a single layer in a baking pan, and toast in a 350°F-oven for 10 to 15 minutes, until the skins begin to blister. Pour the nuts onto a clean dish towel, wrap the towel around the nuts, and let them steam for a minute or two. Use the towel to rub the skins off the nuts (some bits may stick, which is fine).

Savory

Recipes

PART THREE

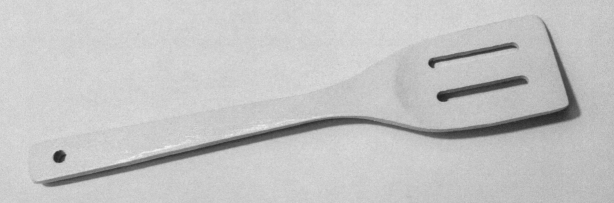

7

SAVORY BREADS and SNACKS

I find bread baking to be one of the most satisfying types of baking. Sure, you don't get the same level of appreciation and awe that you get when you make pies and cakes, but if you can turn out a loaf of perfectly baked homemade bread, you know you have mastered a practical life skill. This chapter includes yeasted breads, quick breads, and treats like homemade pretzels and other savory snacks your friends and loved ones are sure to appreciate.

BUTTERMILK SANDWICH BREAD

Prep time: 20 MINUTES, PLUS 1 HOUR TO RISE AND 1 HOUR TO COOL   *Cook time:* 35 MINUTES
Makes: 1 LOAF (ABOUT 14 SLICES)

LEVEL

NUT-FREE

EQUIPMENT
Large mixing bowl with electric mixer or stand mixer, small saucepan, 9-by-5-by-3-inch loaf pan, clean dish towel

3¼ cups bread flour or all-purpose flour, divided

1 tablespoon sugar

1 teaspoon salt

2¼ teaspoons (1 envelope) active dry yeast or instant yeast

1¼ cups buttermilk

3 tablespoons unsalted butter, divided, plus more for greasing

1 egg

With just a few ingredients, this sandwich bread is a good intro to bread making. The buttermilk adds a nice tang, and this bread turns out soft and light, like classic white bread. It's a great choice for making all types of sandwiches—whether you're in the mood for PB&J, ham and cheese, or egg salad. It makes nice toast for breakfast, too.

1. MAKE THE DOUGH. In the bowl of a stand mixer or in a large mixing bowl using an electric mixer, combine 1½ cups of flour with the sugar, salt, and yeast. In a small saucepan over medium heat, heat the buttermilk and 2 tablespoons of butter until the butter is melted and the mixture is warm but not boiling. Add the warm buttermilk mixture to the flour mixture, and beat to combine well. Add the egg and beat just to incorporate, about 1 more minute. Add the remaining 1¾ cups of flour, and beat for 5 minutes more.

2. KNEAD THE DOUGH. Transfer the dough to a lightly floured work surface and knead it for 2 minutes. The dough will be fairly sticky.

3. FORM THE LOAF. Butter the loaf pan. Form the dough into a loaf shape, and place it in the pan. Melt the remaining 1 tablespoon of butter, and brush it over the loaf. Cover the dough loosely with a clean dish towel and set in a warm spot (like your kitchen countertop) to rise for about 1 hour. The dough should rise up over the top of the pan.

4. BAKE THE BREAD AND SERVE. Preheat the oven to 375°F. Using a sharp knife, cut a ½-inch-deep slash lengthwise down the dough. This helps keep the shape as the bread bakes. Bake in the preheated oven for about 35 minutes, until the crust is lightly browned. Let cool in the pan on a wire rack for 10 minutes. Remove from the loaf pan and let cool to room temperature before slicing and serving.

EASY CHEESY BREAD

Prep time: 15 MINUTES, PLUS 15 MINUTES TO COOL   *Cook time:* 20 MINUTES
Makes: 1 LOAF (ABOUT 12 SLICES)

LEVEL

NUT-FREE

EQUIPMENT
Baking sheet, parchment paper, large mixing bowl, wooden spoon

1¾ cups all-purpose flour, plus more for dusting

2½ teaspoons baking powder

1 teaspoon salt

1 cup plain Greek yogurt

¼ cup olive oil

4 ounces cheese (Asiago, Cheddar, or another firm cheese), cut into ½-inch dice

This may be the easiest bread recipe you'll ever find. Instead of using yeast to give it rise, it combines Greek yogurt (an acidic ingredient) with baking powder (which is activated by acid). I love loading this bread up with a strong-flavored cheese like Asiago, but you can substitute any firm cheese you like—Cheddar, Gruyère, or Gouda would all be great choices. This bread is delightful toasted, made into a sandwich (try a BLT, turkey and avocado, or roasted veggies), or alongside eggs for breakfast.

1. **PREHEAT THE OVEN AND PREPARE THE PAN.** Preheat the oven to 400°F. Line a baking sheet with parchment paper.

2. **MIX THE DOUGH.** In a large mixing bowl, stir together the flour, baking powder, and salt. Add the yogurt and olive oil, and stir with a wooden spoon until the mixture comes together to form a ball. Add the cheese, and mix it in with your hands so the cubes are well distributed throughout the dough.

3. **FORM THE DOUGH.** Transfer the dough ball to a lightly floured work surface and shape it into a loaf shape, about 8 inches long. Place the loaf on the prepared baking sheet. Make a few diagonal slashes in the top of the loaf.

4. **BAKE THE BREAD AND SERVE.** Bake in the preheated oven for 20 minutes, until the crust is golden brown. Let cool for at least 15 minutes before slicing. Serve warm or at room temperature.

JALAPEÑO CORNBREAD

Prep time: 10 MINUTES   *Cook time:* 25 MINUTES   *Serves:* 8

LEVEL 1

NUT-FREE

EQUIPMENT
8-inch square cake pan, large mixing bowl, whisk, medium mixing bowl

¼ cup (½ stick) unsalted butter, melted, plus more for greasing

1¼ cups cornmeal

1 cup all-purpose flour

½ cup granulated sugar

1 tablespoon baking powder

½ teaspoon salt

1 cup (whole or low-fat) milk

1 egg

1 cup fresh or frozen corn kernels

1 jalapeño pepper, seeded and diced

Cornbread makes a great side dish for soup or chili, but it is also great as a snack on its own. Most of the jalapeño's heat is in the seeds and ribs, so by removing these, you can keep the bread from being too spicy. Wear gloves while handling the jalapeño pepper. If you rub your eyes even an hour or two after cutting it, they may start to burn and be very uncomfortable.

1. **PREHEAT THE OVEN AND PREPARE THE BAKING PAN.** Preheat the oven to 400°F. Grease the cake pan with butter.

2. **MIX THE DRY INGREDIENTS.** In a large mixing bowl, whisk together the cornmeal, flour, sugar, baking powder, and salt until evenly combined.

3. **ADD THE WET INGREDIENTS.** In a medium mixing bowl, whisk together the milk and egg. Add the wet mixture to the dry mixture, and stir until combined. Stir in the corn and jalapeño.

4. **BAKE THE CORNBREAD AND SERVE.** Transfer the batter to the prepared cake pan and bake in the preheated oven for 20 to 25 minutes, until the crust is golden brown. Serve warm or at room temperature.

OLIVE BREAD TWISTS

Prep time: 25 MINUTES, PLUS 2 HOURS AND 10 MINUTES TO PROOF AND RISE   *Cook time:* 15 MINUTES
Makes: ABOUT 12 BREAD TWISTS

LEVEL

NUT-FREE
DAIRY-FREE

EQUIPMENT
Large mixing bowl with electric mixer or stand mixer, clean dish towel, baking sheet, parchment paper, pastry brush

1 cup warm water

1 teaspoon granulated sugar

1 teaspoon active dry yeast

2 cups all-purpose flour

¼ cup olive oil, plus more for brushing

¼ teaspoon salt

¼ cup chopped olives

Crunchy breadsticks are great for dunking into a bowl of tomato soup or accompanying a bowl of stew instead of cornbread or dinner rolls. For even more flavor, try kneading in chopped garlic and herbs along with the olives, or sprinkle them with freshly grated Parmesan cheese as soon as they come out of the oven.

1. PROOF THE YEAST. In a large mixing bowl or the bowl of a stand mixer, combine the warm water, sugar, and yeast. Let stand for about 10 minutes, until the mixture becomes foamy.

2. MAKE THE DOUGH. Add the flour and olive oil, and mix until well combined. Add the salt, and knead by hand for about 10 minutes or using the dough hook on a stand mixer for 5 minutes. Add the olives, and knead them into the dough until they are well incorporated.

3. LET RISE. Press the dough out into a rectangle about 9 by 4 inches. Cover with a clean dish towel and let rise in a warm spot in your kitchen for about 2 hours until about doubled in size.

4. PREHEAT THE OVEN AND MAKE THE TWISTS. Preheat the oven to 400°F. Line a baking sheet with parchment paper. Use a sharp knife to cut the dough into strips about 4 inches long and 1 inch wide. Roll the strips into ropes about 9 inches long. Twist each rope, and lay them on the prepared baking sheet. Brush the tops with olive oil.

5. BAKE AND SERVE. Bake in the preheated oven for about 15 minutes, until light golden brown. Transfer the bread twists to a wire rack to cool completely before serving.

CHEESY STRAWS

Prep time: 15 MINUTES, PLUS 20 MINUTES TO CHILL THE DOUGH   *Cook time:* 30 MINUTES
Makes: ABOUT 48 STRAWS

LEVEL

NUT-FREE

EQUIPMENT
Large mixing bowl with an electric mixer or stand mixer, parchment paper, rolling pin, baking sheet

½ cup (1 stick) unsalted butter, at room temperature

2½ cups shredded firm cheese (Swiss, Gruyère, Asiago, or Cheddar)

1⅔ cups all-purpose flour

1 teaspoon salt

2 tablespoons water

Munch these fancy-looking treats with your friends as an afterschool or movie-night snack. You can make these in about an hour and serve them with a main course or as an accompaniment to a big salad, as well.

1. MIX THE DOUGH. In the bowl of a stand mixer or in a large mixing bowl using an electric mixer, beat together the butter and cheese. Add the flour and salt in 3 batches, beating on low after each addition, until combined. Add the water and beat to incorporate, about 1 more minute.

2. ROLL OUT THE DOUGH. Transfer the dough to a lightly floured work surface, and knead it 4 or 5 times. On a large piece of parchment paper, use a rolling pin to roll the dough out into a 12-by-9-inch rectangle. Lift the dough on the parchment paper, and lay it on a baking sheet. Chill in the refrigerator for 20 minutes.

3. PREHEAT THE OVEN, BAKE THE CHEESE STRAWS, AND SERVE. Preheat the oven to 425°F. Cut the rectangle of dough into 2 (6-by-9-inch) rectangles. Return one of the rectangles to the refrigerator. Using a sharp knife, starting from one of the short sides, cut the dough into ¼-inch-by-6-inch strips. Arrange the strips on the baking sheet, leaving about half an inch of space in between. Bake in the preheated oven for about 15 minutes, until the straws are crisp and golden. Remove from the oven and transfer to a wire rack to cool completely. Repeat with the second rectangle of dough while the first is baking, and then bake the second batch of straws. Serve warm.

HONEY-WHEAT SESAME CRACKERS

Prep time: 20 MINUTES   *Cook time:* 10 MINUTES   *Makes:* ABOUT 48 CRACKERS

LEVEL

NUT-FREE

EQUIPMENT

Large mixing bowl with pastry cutter (or two knives) or food processor, rolling pin, parchment paper, baking sheet, pizza cutter or sharp knife

1¼ cups whole-wheat flour, plus more for rolling

½ teaspoon salt

¼ cup cold, unsalted butter, cut into small pieces

1½ tablespoons honey

¼ cup water

2 tablespoons sesame seeds

Salt, for sprinkling

It's true: You can make your own crackers! And once you do, you may never want to buy crackers at the store again. These come out perfectly crisp and crunchy every time. Substitute different seeds—think pumpkin, flax, or sunflower seed—if you like.

1. MAKE THE DOUGH. In a large mixing bowl or the bowl of a food processor, combine the flour and salt. Using the food processor, a pastry cutter, or two knives, cut the butter into the flour until it forms pea-size lumps. Add the honey, water, and sesame seeds and mix until the mixture comes together in a soft dough.

2. PREHEAT THE OVEN TO 400°F.

3. ROLL OUT THE DOUGH AND CUT THE CRACKERS. Lay a piece of parchment paper large enough to cover your baking sheet on the counter, and dust it lightly with flour. Using a quarter of the dough at a time, use a rolling pin to roll it out on the parchment paper until it is as thin and even as you can get it and still handle it. Slide the parchment paper with the dough onto a baking sheet. With a pizza cutter or sharp knife, very gently cut the dough into cracker shapes (you can make rectangles, squares, triangles, or whatever shape you wish). Sprinkle salt over the crackers.

4. BAKE THE CRACKERS AND SERVE. Bake the crackers in the preheated oven for 6 to 9 minutes, until they are golden brown and crisp. Remove the baking sheet from the oven, and slide the parchment paper onto a wire rack. Let the crackers cool. Serve at room temperature.

GIANT SOFT PRETZELS

Prep time: 20 MINUTES, PLUS 45 MINUTES FOR DOUGH TO REST/RISE *Cook time:* 10 MINUTES
Makes: 8 LARGE PRETZELS

LEVEL

NUT-FREE

EQUIPMENT

Large mixing bowl with electric mixer or wooden spoon or stand mixer, clean dish towel, 9-inch square baking dish, whisk, baking sheet, parchment paper, pastry brush

FOR THE DOUGH

2½ cups all-purpose flour

1 teaspoon salt

1 teaspoon sugar

2¼ teaspoons (1 envelope) instant yeast

1 cup warm water

Nonstick cooking spray

FOR THE BAKING SODA BATH

1 cup boiling water

2 tablespoons baking soda

FOR TOPPING

Coarse salt, for sprinkling

3 tablespoons unsalted butter, melted

Learn how to bake those wonderful soft pretzels found at street vendors, movie theaters, and mall food courts everywhere. The secret to getting that shiny, chewy pretzel exterior is to soak the dough in a "bath" of water and baking soda—it's also what gives them that beautiful golden-brown color. Top them with a sprinkling of coarse salt, or try a mixture of poppy seeds, sesame seeds, garlic salt, and onion salt to create an "everything" bagel–flavored pretzel. Or go sweet and sprinkle them with cinnamon and sugar after slathering on the melted butter.

1. **MAKE THE DOUGH.** In a large mixing bowl or the bowl of a stand mixer, combine the flour, salt, sugar, yeast, and warm water, and beat with an electric mixer or a wooden spoon to mix. Knead the dough until smooth, about 5 minutes with an electric mixer or 10 minutes by hand. Sprinkle the dough with a bit of flour, and cover it with a clean dish towel. Let rise for about 30 minutes.

2. **PREPARE THE BAKING SODA BATH.** Put the boiling water in the baking dish and add the baking soda, whisking until the baking soda dissolves. Let cool.

3. **PREHEAT THE OVEN AND PREPARE THE PAN.** Preheat the oven to 475°F. Line a baking sheet with parchment paper or spray it with cooking spray.

4. FORM THE PRETZELS. Spray your work surface lightly with cooking spray. Transfer the dough to the work surface, and divide it into 8 equal-size balls. Let the dough balls rest, uncovered, for 5 minutes. Roll each ball between your palms (or between your palms and the work surface) into a long, thin rope about 28 inches long. Twist each rope into the classic twisted pretzel shape, pressing the ends down to seal them. Place each of the pretzels, one at a time, in the baking soda bath. Make sure the pretzel is completely submerged, and let sit in the bath for a couple of minutes. Place the soaked pretzels on the prepared baking sheet, and sprinkle them with the salt. Let the formed pretzels rest on the baking sheet, uncovered, for 10 minutes.

5. BAKE THE PRETZELS AND SERVE. Bake the pretzels in the preheated oven for 8 to 10 minutes, until golden brown all over. Remove the baking sheet from the oven and immediately brush the tops of the pretzels with the melted butter. Let cool slightly and serve hot.

PIGS IN PUFFS

Prep time: 15 MINUTES, PLUS 15 MINUTES TO CHILL   *Cook time:* 30 MINUTES   *Makes:* 16

LEVEL 2

NUT-FREE

EQUIPMENT
Rolling pin, large baking sheet, parchment paper, pastry brush

Flour, for dusting

2 sheets frozen puff pastry, thawed according to package directions

2 tablespoons Dijon mustard, plus more for serving

8 hot dogs or sausages, halved widthwise

1 egg, lightly beaten

The traditional pigs-in-a-blanket dish is made more special by using puff pastry dough instead of a store-bought crescent dough roll. Use all-beef hot dogs, chicken dogs, fancy sausages, or even tofu dogs for these. Serve them at a weekend sleepover or bring them to a pot luck. They will disappear quickly!

1. PREPARE THE DOUGH. On a lightly floured work surface, use a rolling pin to roll out each sheet of pastry to a 20-by-12-inch rectangle. Cut each sheet into 2 (10-by-12-inch) rectangles, then cut each of those into 4 equal size strips. Cut each strip diagonally into 2 triangles. Repeat with the other puff pastry sheet. You should end up with 16 triangles of dough.

2. PREHEAT THE OVEN AND PREPARE THE PAN. Preheat the oven to 350°F. Line a large baking sheet with parchment paper.

3. FORM THE PUFFS. With the short side of the dough triangle facing you, spread a bit of mustard onto the dough. Top with a hot dog half, and roll the dough around it. Brush a bit of the beaten egg on the pointed tip of the dough, and press to seal the dough. Arrange the rolls on the prepared baking sheet. Chill them in the refrigerator for about 15 minutes.

4. BAKE THE PUFFS AND SERVE. Prick the tops of the rolls with the tines of a fork, and brush the remaining egg wash over the tops. Bake in the preheated oven until the rolls are crisp and golden brown, 25 to 30 minutes. Remove from the oven and serve warm with extra mustard for dipping.

BACON-CHEDDAR CHEESE PUFFS

Prep time: 20 MINUTES, PLUS 10 MINUTES TO COOL THE DOUGH   *Cook time:* 25 MINUTES
Makes: ABOUT 32 CHEESE PUFFS

LEVEL

NUT-FREE

EQUIPMENT

Large skillet, paper towel-lined plate, 2 baking sheets, parchment paper, medium saucepan, wooden spoon, large mixing bowl, electric mixer (or wooden spoon), small cookie scoop

4 slices thick-cut bacon

½ cup water

½ cup (whole or low-fat) milk

½ cup unsalted butter

¾ teaspoon salt

1 cup all-purpose flour

4 eggs

1 cup shredded Cheddar cheese

The base for these delicious puffs is called *pate a choux* (pronounced paht-ah-SHOO), a classically light French pastry used to make bakery favorites like éclairs and profiteroles. When these bake, the moisture turns to steam and the pastry puffs up. Cheese puffs make a nice appetizer to serve before dinner or snack on later. Or cut them in half and place a little tuna or egg salad between the slices for a lovely lunch.

1. COOK THE BACON. In a large skillet over medium heat, cook the bacon until browned and crisp, about 5 minutes. Transfer to a paper towel–lined plate. Let cool, and then crumble or chop into small pieces.

2. PREHEAT THE OVEN AND PREPARE THE PANS. Preheat the oven to 400°F. Line 2 baking sheets with parchment paper.

3. MAKE THE DOUGH. In a medium saucepan over medium heat, stir together the water, milk, butter, and salt and bring to a boil. Add the flour and cook, stirring with a wooden spoon, until the dough comes together in a ball, 1 to 2 minutes. Remove the pan from the heat, and transfer the dough to a large mixing bowl. Let cool for about 10 minutes.

4. BEAT IN THE EGGS. Add the eggs to the dough one at a time, beating with an electric mixer or wooden spoon after each addition until thoroughly combined. Add the bacon and cheese, and beat to combine.

5. FORM THE PUFFS. Using a small cookie scoop or your hands, form the dough into 1½-inch balls and arrange them on the prepared baking sheets, leaving about 2 inches between the balls.

6. BAKE THE PUFFS AND SERVE. Bake in the preheated oven for 22 to 24 minutes, until the puffs are golden brown. Rotate the pans halfway through baking. Cool slightly on the pan, and then serve warm.

 Tip

These cheese puffs freeze well. Let them cool to room temperature, then freeze them on a baking sheet until frozen solid. Transfer to resealable plastic bags and store in the freezer for up to 3 months. To serve, reheat the puffs from frozen in a 350°F oven for 10 minutes.

8

SAVORY
PIES, TARTS,
and PIZZA

Making dessert pies is sort of an easy trick. It's no surprise that everyone goes gaga over a pastry filled with sweet fruit, cooked to syrupy deliciousness. But a savory pie or tart? That's where you really knock people's socks off, simply because they aren't expecting to love dinner so much. From homemade pizza to chicken pot pie, these savory baked dishes are sure to win you fans.

CHICKEN POT PIE

Prep time: 30 MINUTES, PLUS 1 HOUR TO CHILL THE DOUGH   *Cook time:* 45 MINUTES
Makes: 4 INDIVIDUAL POT PIES

LEVEL 2

NUT-FREE

EQUIPMENT

Food processor or large mixing bowl with pastry cutter (or two knives), plastic wrap, baking sheet, aluminum foil, 4 (8-ounce) ramekins, large saucepan or skillet, small mixing bowl, whisk, ladle, rolling pin, skewer or toothpick

FOR THE CRUST

2½ cups all-purpose flour, plus more for rolling

½ teaspoon salt

1 cup plus 2 tablespoons cold, unsalted butter, cut into ½-inch pieces

4 to 7 tablespoons ice water or more, if needed

When I was a kid, my first chicken pot pie came from a supermarket freezer and I thought it was one of the best things I had ever eaten. When I tasted my first homemade chicken pot pie, I was head over heels. And, needless to say, these freeze well, so you can have a homemade pot pie whenever you have a craving.

1. **MAKE THE DOUGH.** In the bowl of a food processor or in a large mixing bowl, mix together the flour and salt. Add the cold butter pieces and pulse, if using the food processor, or cut into the flour with a pastry cutter or two knives until the mixture is in pea-size clumps. Add the ice water, 2 tablespoons at a time, and pulse or mix just until the dough comes together in a ball (you may not need to use all the water). Roll the dough into a ball, then flatten it into a disk shape. Wrap it tightly in plastic wrap, and chill in the refrigerator for at least an hour.

2. **PREHEAT THE OVEN AND PREPARE THE PANS.** Preheat the oven to 425°F. Line a baking sheet with aluminum foil, and arrange 4 (8-ounce) ramekins on it.

FOR THE FILLING

2 tablespoons olive oil

1 onion, diced

2 carrots, diced

2 large celery stalks, diced

1 ¾ cups chicken broth
or water

1 ½ cups chopped
cooked chicken

1 cup frozen peas

1 teaspoon salt

2 teaspoons chopped fresh
thyme leaves

¾ cup (whole or low-fat) milk

¼ cup all-purpose flour

3. MAKE THE FILLING. In a large saucepan or skillet over medium heat, heat the olive oil. Add the onion, carrots, and celery and cook, stirring frequently, until soft, about 8 minutes. Add the chicken broth (or water), chicken, peas, salt, and thyme, and bring to a boil. In a small mixing bowl, whisk together the milk and flour until smooth and stir into the chicken mixture. Cook, stirring, until the sauce thickens, about 5 minutes more. Remove from the heat, and ladle the mixture into the ramekins.

4. ROLL OUT THE DOUGH. Use a rolling pin on a lightly floured work surface to roll out the dough into a rectangle about ⅛ inch thick. Using one of the ramekins as a guide, cut out 4 circles, each about 3 inches wider than the ramekins. Place one dough circle on top of each filled ramekin, then poke several holes in the top of the dough with a skewer or toothpick. Transfer the ramekins on the baking sheet to the oven.

5. BAKE THE POT PIES AND SERVE. Bake in the preheated oven for about 30 minutes, until the filling is bubbling and the crust is golden brown. Remove from the oven and let cool for a few minutes before serving.

PESTO AND TURKEY TOASTER PASTRIES

Prep time: 30 MINUTES, PLUS 1 HOUR TO CHILL THE DOUGH   *Cook time:* 30 MINUTES   *Makes:* 8 PIES

LEVEL

EQUIPMENT

Food processor or large mixing bowl with pastry cutter (or two knives), plastic wrap, 2 large rimmed baking sheets, parchment paper, rolling pin, pastry brush, skewer or toothpick

FOR THE CRUST

2½ cups all-purpose flour, plus more for rolling

½ teaspoon salt

1 cup plus 2 tablespoons cold, unsalted butter, cut into ½-inch pieces

4 to 7 tablespoons ice water or more, if needed

FOR THE FILLING

¼ cup pesto

8 ounces sliced deli turkey

5 ounces fontina or mozzarella cheese, cut into 8 pieces

1 egg, beaten with 1 tablespoon cold water, as an egg wash

I love baking up these cute little handheld pies. They are terrific served warm from the oven, but they are equally delish eaten at room temperature, so go ahead and make a bunch of these to pack for lunch.

1. MAKE THE DOUGH. In the bowl of a food processor or in a large mixing bowl, mix together the flour and salt. Add the cold butter pieces and pulse, if using the food processor, or cut into the flour with a pastry cutter or two knives, until the mixture is in pea-size clumps. Add the ice water, 2 tablespoons at a time, and pulse or mix just until the dough comes together in a ball (you may not need to use all the water). Roll the dough into a ball, then flatten it into a disk shape. Wrap it tightly in plastic wrap, and chill in the refrigerator for at least an hour.

2. PREHEAT THE OVEN AND PREPARE THE BAKING PANS. Preheat the oven to 375°F. Line the baking sheets with parchment paper.

3. ROLL OUT THE DOUGH. Split the dough into two equal pieces. On a lightly floured work surface, use a rolling pin to roll out each piece of dough into a 13-by-11-inch rectangle about ⅛ inch thick. Trim the edges so that the sides are straight, then cut each sheet into 8 (5-by-3-inch) rectangles. You should have 16 rectangles.

4. ASSEMBLE THE PASTRIES. Arrange 8 of the rectangles on the prepared baking sheets, leaving at least an inch of space between them. Dollop about 1½ teaspoons of pesto onto each rectangle and spread it down the center, leaving a border of at least half an inch. Divide the turkey evenly among the rectangles. Add the cheese on top of the turkey, dividing equally. Brush the edges of the dough with a bit of the egg wash. Top each stack with one of the remaining 8 dough rectangles. Use the tines of a fork to seal the edges and make a decorative border all the way around each rectangle. With a skewer or toothpick, prick several holes in the top of each pastry. Brush the remaining egg wash on top of the pastries.

5. BAKE THE PIES AND SERVE. Place the baking sheets in the preheated oven and bake for 25 to 30 minutes until the crusts are golden brown. Transfer the pastries to a wire rack to cool. Serve immediately or let cool to room temperature before serving.

CRUSTLESS QUICHE

WITH SUN-DRIED TOMATO, BACON, AND GOAT CHEESE

Prep time: 15 MINUTES   *Cook time:* 1 HOUR   *Serves:* 6

LEVEL **1**

NUT-FREE
GLUTEN-FREE

EQUIPMENT
Medium skillet, paper towel–lined plate, 9-inch pie plate, large mixing bowl, whisk

¼ pound bacon

Nonstick cooking spray

4 eggs

1 cup (whole or low-fat) milk

½ cup sun-dried tomatoes, drained and chopped

¼ cup freshly grated Parmesan cheese

¼ teaspoon salt

1 cup crumbled goat cheese

Some people don't realize you can make a quiche without the crust, but for those who need to stay away from gluten it's a dream come true. And taking away the need to make a crust cuts down the prep time considerably. The tart-sweet sun-dried tomatoes and salty bacon go together really well. Like any quiche, this is just as good at room temperature as it is warm, so it's an ideal choice for breakfast, brunch, lunch, or dinner at home or to tuck into your lunchbox.

1. COOK THE BACON. In a medium skillet over medium-high heat, cook the bacon until browned and crisp, about 5 minutes. Transfer to a paper towel–lined plate to cool. Crumble the bacon into small pieces and set aside.

2. PREHEAT THE OVEN AND PREPARE THE PAN. Preheat the oven to 350°F. Spray the pie plate with cooking spray.

3. MIX THE FILLING. In a large mixing bowl, whisk together the eggs, milk, sun-dried tomatoes, Parmesan, and salt. Stir in the goat cheese.

4. BAKE THE QUICHE AND SERVE. Transfer the filling mixture to the prepared pie plate, and sprinkle the bacon over the top. Bake in the preheated oven for 50 to 55 minutes, until the top is puffed up and golden brown. Remove from the oven and let cool for a few minutes before slicing into wedges to serve.

BRIE CHEESE
BAKED IN PUFF PASTRY WITH PECANS

Prep time: 10 MINUTES, PLUS 10 MINUTES TO COOL   *Cook time:* 40 MINUTES   *Serves:* 8

LEVEL

EQUIPMENT
Baking sheet, parchment paper, rolling pin, pastry brush, platter

Flour, for dusting

1 sheet frozen puff pastry, thawed according to package directions

1 (8- to 10-ounce) round Brie cheese

½ cup honey, divided

½ cup chopped toasted pecans, divided

1 egg, lightly beaten

1 French baguette, sliced

Sliced apples, for serving

If you are looking for a fancy appetizer, you've found it. Flaky pastry encloses gooey, melty Brie cheese along with sweet honey and nuts. This is one of those great dishes that is super easy to make (thanks, puff pastry!), and super impressive (again, thanks, puff pastry!). Serve this warm from the oven with slices of baguette and apples for scooping up the cheesy mix.

1. **PREHEAT THE OVEN AND PREPARE THE PAN.** Preheat the oven to 400°F. Line a baking sheet with parchment paper.

2. **ROLL OUT THE PASTRY.** On a lightly floured surface, use a rolling pin to roll out the pastry sheet until it is a bit thinner and larger than when it came out of the package.

3. **WRAP THE BRIE.** Place the whole Brie round in the center of the pastry sheet. Drizzle ¼ cup of honey and sprinkle ¼ cup of nuts on top of the Brie. Fold the corners of the pastry up and over the Brie. Press to seal the edges. Using a pastry brush, brush beaten egg over the top and sides of the pastry. Place the wrapped Brie on the prepared baking sheet.

4. **BAKE THE BRIE.** Bake in the preheated oven for 35 to 40 minutes, until the pastry is golden brown and crisp. Remove from the oven and let cool for at least 10 minutes.

5. **GARNISH AND SERVE.** Lift the pastry from the baking sheet using the parchment paper as a sling, and transfer it to a serving platter. Spoon the remaining ¼ cup of honey over the top of the pastry, and sprinkle with the remaining ¼ cup of nuts. Serve immediately with slices of baguette and apples.

BROCCOLI-CHEDDAR TART

Prep time: 30 MINUTES, PLUS 1 HOUR TO CHILL THE DOUGH   *Cook time:* 50 MINUTES   *Serves:* 8

LEVEL

NUT-FREE

EQUIPMENT

Food processor or large mixing bowl with pastry cutter (or two knives), plastic wrap, rolling pin, 9-inch tart pan with removable bottom, parchment paper, pie weights or dried beans, medium saucepan, medium mixing bowl

FOR THE CRUST

1¼ cups all-purpose flour, plus more for rolling

¼ teaspoon salt

½ cup (1 stick) plus 1 tablespoon cold, unsalted butter, cut into ½-inch pieces

2 to 4 tablespoons ice water or more, if needed

FOR THE FILLING

Salt

2 cups chopped broccoli florets

1¼ cups half-and-half

3 eggs

½ teaspoon salt

⅛ teaspoon freshly ground black pepper

Pinch ground nutmeg

1 cup grated sharp Cheddar cheese

This delicate but hearty tart is loaded with a creamy broccoli-and-cheese filling. Like a quiche, it can be served hot or at room temperature, making it a great choice for breakfast or brunch, to pack into a lunch box or take on a picnic, or for an easy make-ahead dinner.

1. MAKE THE DOUGH. In the bowl of a food processor or in a large mixing bowl, mix together the flour and salt. Add the cold butter pieces and pulse, if using the food processor, or cut into the flour with a pastry cutter or two knives, until the mixture is in pea-size clumps. Add 2 tablespoons of ice water, and pulse or mix, adding additional ice water as needed, just until the dough comes together in a ball (you may not need to use all the water). Roll the dough into a ball, then flatten it into a disk shape. Wrap it tightly in plastic wrap and chill in the refrigerator for at least an hour.

2. PREHEAT THE OVEN AND ROLL OUT THE CRUST. First, preheat the oven to 450°F. On a lightly floured work surface, use a rolling pin to roll out the dough into a circle about 14 inches across and ⅛ inch thick. Transfer the dough round to the tart pan by rolling it up onto the rolling pin and then unrolling it over the pan. Trim any excess dough from the edges, leaving about a half-inch overhang. Fold under the overhanging dough, and crimp it all the way around (see page 32).

3. BLIND BAKE THE CRUST. Line the crust with parchment paper and fill with pie weights or dried beans. Bake in the preheated oven for 10 minutes. Lift out the pie weights and parchment, and cook the crust for another 6 to 8 minutes, until golden brown. Remove from the oven and set on a wire rack to cool in the pan. Reduce the oven heat to 350°F.

4. PREPARE THE FILLING. Fill a medium saucepan with lightly salted water and bring to a boil. Add the broccoli and cook for about 4 minutes, until the broccoli is crisp-tender. Drain well and set aside. In a medium mixing bowl, whisk together the half-and-half, eggs, salt, pepper, and nutmeg.

5. FILL THE TART. Spread the par-cooked broccoli in the tart crust. Layer the shredded cheese over the broccoli. Pour the half-and-half mixture over the top.

6. BAKE THE TART AND SERVE. Bake in the preheated oven for 25 to 30 minutes, until the filling is set and beginning to brown. Serve hot or at room temperature.

ITALIAN SPINACH AND CHEESE TART
(TORTA RUSTICA)

Prep time: 15 MINUTES *Cook time:* 50 MINUTES *Serves:* 8

LEVEL **1**

NUT-FREE

EQUIPMENT
9-by-11-inch baking dish, pastry brush, large mixing bowl, whisk

1 tablespoon unsalted butter, melted, plus more for greasing

½ loaf crusty Italian bread, cut into ¼-inch-thick slices

1½ cups shredded fontina cheese, divided

1 (10-ounce) package frozen spinach, thawed, drained, and squeezed dry

¾ cup canned diced roasted red peppers, drained

2 cups half-and-half

6 eggs

1 teaspoon salt

¼ teaspoon freshly ground black pepper

Although this is called a tart, it is similar to a savory bread pudding because it combines crusty bread with a savory custard and lots of cheese. It's perfect for breakfast or brunch, but satisfying enough to stand in as an easy (and filling) dinner, too.

1. PREHEAT THE OVEN AND PREPARE THE BAKING DISH. Preheat the oven to 375°F. Grease the baking dish with butter.

2. MAKE THE CRUST. Lay bread slices in the bottom of the prepared baking dish in a single layer, cutting the slices as needed to fit them in so they completely cover the bottom. Stand bread pieces up against the sides of the dish, too, cutting slices to fit without sticking up over the edge. Using a pastry brush, brush the melted butter over the bread.

3. FILL THE CRUST. Sprinkle about half of the shredded cheese over the bread slices. Top with the spinach, spreading it out in an even layer. Add the peppers in an even layer over the spinach.

4. MAKE THE CUSTARD. In a large mixing bowl, whisk together the half-and-half, eggs, salt, and pepper. Pour this mixture over the vegetables in the baking dish. Sprinkle the remaining cheese over the top.

5. BAKE THE TART AND SERVE. Bake in the preheated oven for about 50 minutes, until the top is golden brown and bubbly. Serve hot.

SPANAKOPITA CUPS

Prep time: 20 MINUTES *Cook time:* 20 MINUTES *Makes:* ABOUT 12 CUPS

<u>LEVEL</u> 2

<u>NUT-FREE</u>

EQUIPMENT
Large mixing bowl, pizza cutter or kitchen shears, 24-cup mini muffin tin, pastry brush

1 (10-ounce) package frozen chopped spinach, thawed and squeezed dry

¾ cup crumbled feta cheese

½ cup sour cream

2 eggs, lightly beaten

2 scallions, thinly sliced

2 tablespoons chopped fresh dill

2 garlic cloves, minced

½ teaspoon salt

¼ teaspoon freshly ground black pepper

1 (16-ounce) package frozen phyllo dough, thawed

6 tablespoons unsalted butter, melted

Spanakopita is a Greek savory pastry stuffed with spinach and feta cheese. The pastry shell is made with phyllo, multiple layers of very thin sheets of dough that are layered on top of each other with melted butter or olive oil in between. Phyllo bakes up into an almost supernaturally crisp crust. I've created an easier version here that uses the phyllo as a crust in muffin cups with the filling spooned on top. Look for phyllo dough in the supermarket freezer alongside puff pastry and pie crust. A 16-ounce package usually contains about 40 sheets of phyllo. These paper-thin sheets are delicate, but as long as you are gentle with them and follow instructions, you'll do just fine. Serve these cute little cups at a weekend brunch, casual party, or late-night snack session.

1. **MAKE THE FILLING.** In a large mixing bowl, stir together the spinach, feta, sour cream, eggs, scallions, dill, garlic, salt, and pepper, mixing well.

2. **FORM THE PHYLLO CUPS.** Remove the phyllo dough from the package, carefully unroll the dough, and stack about 3 sheets on top of each other. Using a pizza cutter or kitchen shears, cut the sheets into 2-inch squares. Brush melted butter into each well of a mini muffin tin. Stack 2 of the square phyllo sheets in each well, pressing them into the well to create a cup. Brush more butter on top of the phyllo. Add 2 more square phyllo sheets into each well, pressing them down into the cup and then brushing with butter. Repeat once more with 2 more square phyllo sheets in each well (you'll have a total of 6 layers of phyllo in each cup). Brush with the remaining butter.

3. **FILL AND BAKE THE PHYLLO CUPS AND SERVE.** Preheat the oven to 375°F. Spoon the spinach mixture into the phyllo cups, filling each well. Bake in the preheated oven for 15 to 20 minutes, until the phyllo is golden brown. Serve immediately.

CLASSIC THIN-CRUST PIZZA

Prep time: 15 MINUTES, PLUS 1 HOUR AND 10 MINUTES FOR DOUGH TO PROOF AND RISE
Cook time: 15 MINUTES   *Makes:* 1 (14-INCH) PIZZA

LEVEL

NUT-FREE

EQUIPMENT
Two large mixing bowls; electric mixer, stand mixer, or wooden spoon; clean dish towel, rolling pin, baking sheet

¾ cup very warm water

2¼ teaspoons (1 envelope) instant yeast

½ teaspoon granulated sugar

1 tablespoon olive oil, plus more for oiling

1 cup whole-wheat flour

1 cup all-purpose flour

1 teaspoon salt

1 cup pizza sauce

1 cup (about 4 ounces) shredded mozzarella cheese or an Italian cheese mix

½ teaspoon dried oregano

Here is a basic recipe for classic cheese pizza. Once you make it a couple of times, change things up by adding different toppings. You can divide the dough into 2 individual-size pizzas and set up bowls of assorted toppings to let your dinner guests create their own personal pizza. Be careful not to put too many toppings on each pizza, though, or the dough will end up soggy since it will absorb excess water.

1. PROOF THE DOUGH. In a large mixing bowl, stir together the warm water, yeast, and sugar. Let the mixture stand for about 10 minutes, until it becomes foamy. Stir in the olive oil.

2. MIX THE DOUGH. Add both flours and the salt to the yeast mixture, with an electric mixer, stand mixer, or wooden spoon, until the dough is well combined and comes together in a ball. Knead the dough either by hand for 3 or 4 minutes or with a mixer for 1 to 2 minutes.

3. LET THE DOUGH RISE. Grease a large mixing bowl lightly with olive oil. Place the dough ball in the bowl, and turn it over once to coat with oil. Cover with a clean dish towel and let the dough rise in a warm spot on your countertop until doubled in size, about 1 hour.

4. PREHEAT THE OVEN AND FORM AND PAR BAKE THE CRUST.
Preheat the oven to 500°F. On a lightly floured work surface, use a rolling pin to roll out the dough as thin as you can get it. You can also try stretching the pizza dough on your hands like they do in pizzerias, but hold off on throwing it in the air until you've had plenty of practice. Place the dough on a baking sheet and bake in the preheated oven for about 5 minutes, until it is just lightly colored. Remove from the oven. »

5. TOP THE PIZZA. Spread the sauce over the crust, leaving a 1-inch clear border around the outside. Sprinkle the cheese over the sauce in an even layer, then sprinkle on the oregano.

6. BAKE THE PIZZA AND SERVE. Bake the pizza in the preheated oven for 6 to 8 minutes, until the crust bubbles up and turns golden brown and the cheese is melted and bubbling. Serve hot.

Tip

If you want to get a head start, you can make the pizza dough through step 3 above and then wrap it in a lightly oiled piece of plastic wrap and store it in the refrigerator for up to 2 days. Bring it to room temperature by letting it sit out on the countertop for 30 minutes before using. To freeze the dough, divide it into 2 balls and wrap tightly in plastic wrap. Place them in a resealable freezer bag and freeze for up to 3 months. Thaw the dough in the refrigerator overnight and bring to room temperature before using.

5 WAYS TO USE PIZZA DOUGH (OTHER THAN PIZZA)

Once you discover how easy it is to make pizza dough from scratch, you'll probably find yourself making it often. Here are my favorite ways to use pizza dough besides the obvious. Bake each of these in a 500°F oven for 15 to 20 minutes.

Cheesy Bread Sticks: Roll out the dough, cut it into strips, and top the strips with melted butter and shredded cheese. Bake until golden brown.

Egg and Cheese Bread: Roll out the dough, top it with scrambled eggs and cheese, and then fold the sides over to enclose the filling. Brush with an egg wash (see page 62) and bake until golden brown.

Pizza Taco Cups: Press small balls of dough into a muffin tin to make cups. Fill with refried beans and cooked seasoned taco meat. Top with cheese and bake until the crusts are golden brown.

Chili Cheese Pizza Dogs: Roll out the dough, and cut it into 8 rectangles. Top each with a hot dog and a dollop of chili. Sprinkle cheese over the hot dogs and chili, and roll the dough up around them like pigs in a blanket. Bake until the crust is golden brown.

Easy Cinnamon Rolls: Roll out the dough into 1 large rectangle. Brush with melted butter, then sprinkle generously with cinnamon sugar. Roll the dough up, starting with one of the long sides, into a tight cylinder. Cut into 2-inch-wide rounds and arrange them, cut-side down, in a buttered baking dish and bake until golden brown.

SAUSAGE AND CHEESE CALZONE

Prep time: 20 MINUTES, PLUS 1 HOUR AND 10 MINUTES FOR YEAST TO PROOF AND DOUGH TO RISE
Cook time: 25 MINUTES *Makes:* 4 CALZONES

LEVEL

NUT-FREE

EQUIPMENT
Two large mixing bowls; electric mixer, stand mixer, or wooden spoon; large mixing bowl; clean dish towel; large skillet; spatula; medium bowl; large baking sheet; parchment paper; rolling pin, pastry brush

2 cups warm (almost hot) water

2¼ teaspoons (1 envelope) instant yeast

2 teaspoons granulated sugar

1 tablespoon olive oil, plus more for oiling

3 cups whole-wheat flour

3 cups all-purpose flour

2 teaspoons salt

1 pound bulk Italian sausage (sweet or spicy)

2 cups pizza sauce

1½ cups shredded mozzarella cheese or an Italian cheese mix

1 teaspoon dried oregano

1 egg, lightly beaten with 1 tablespoon of water

Calzones are basically inside-out pizzas. They're stuffed with the same types of toppings you'd put on a pizza, including cheese and sauce, and then baked. Personalize your calzones with any ingredients you like. This recipe makes 4 large calzones, but it's fun to divide the dough in half again to make 8 small ones and fill them with different things. They're delicious right out of the oven, but they're also great at room temperature, so pack these for lunch anytime.

1. PROOF THE YEAST. In a large mixing bowl, stir together the hot water, yeast, and sugar. Let the mixture stand for about 10 minutes, until it becomes foamy. Stir in the olive oil.

2. MIX THE DOUGH. Add both flours and the salt to the yeast mixture, and mix with an electric mixer, stand mixer, or wooden spoon, until the dough is well combined and comes together in a ball. Knead the dough with the mixer for 1 to 2 minutes or by hand for 3 or 4 minutes.

3. LET THE DOUGH RISE. Grease a large mixing bowl lightly with olive oil. Place the dough ball in the bowl, and turn it over once to coat with oil. Cover with a clean dish towel and let the dough rise in a warm spot on your countertop until doubled in size, about an hour.

4. MAKE THE FILLING. Heat a large skillet over medium-high heat. Add the sausage and cook, stirring and breaking up with a spatula, until the meat is browned, about 5 minutes. Drain off any excess fat. Transfer the meat to a medium bowl and let cool to room temperature. Add the sauce, cheese, and oregano to the meat, and stir to combine.

5. PREHEAT THE OVEN AND FORM THE CALZONE. Preheat the oven to 500°F. Line a large baking sheet with parchment paper. Split the dough into four equal pieces, and use a rolling pin to roll out each piece into about a 7-inch circle. Divide the filling mixture equally among the four dough circles, piling it on one half of the circle and leaving a clear border for sealing the dough. Brush a bit of the beaten egg mixture onto the edges of the circles. Fold the other half of the circle over the filling, and pinch the edges to seal the dough.

6. BAKE THE CALZONE AND SERVE. Transfer the calzone to the prepared baking sheet. Brush the tops of the calzone with the beaten egg mixture. Bake in the preheated oven for 15 to 20 minutes, until the crust is crisp and golden brown. Remove from the oven and serve immediately.

EASY DINNERS

Being able to put a bunch of ingredients in a baking dish, pop it into the oven, and have a delicious meal in an hour is a skill that will get you very far in life. The recipes here are a hit on every level—they are hearty, satisfying, budget-friendly, and nutritious. But be warned, your parents might start expecting you to cook dinner for them every night.

CHICKEN NACHOS

Prep time: 15 MINUTES   *Cook time:* 15 MINUTES   *Serves:* 8

LEVEL 1

NUT-FREE
GLUTEN-FREE

EQUIPMENT
Large mixing bowl, 9-by-13-inch baking dish

1 pound shredded cooked chicken

1 cup salsa, plus more for garnish

1 tablespoon chili powder

2 teaspoons ground cumin

1 teaspoon dried oregano

1 (15-ounce) can refried beans, divided

1 large bag corn tortilla chips, divided

3 cups shredded cheese, divided

¼ cup jalapeño slices from a jar, drained

¼ cup chopped pitted black olives

½ cup sour cream

Fresh cilantro, for garnish (optional)

Snack food doesn't get any better than this. I like to use a mix of sharp Cheddar and mellow Jack cheese, but feel free to use whatever hard cheese suits you. If you like it really spicy, buy hot salsa instead of mild. Nachos are perfect for any casual occasion, but it's hard to beat them on movie night.

1. **SEASON THE CHICKEN.** In a large mixing bowl, toss together the shredded chicken with the salsa, chili powder, cumin, and oregano.

2. **ASSEMBLE THE NACHOS.** Preheat the oven to 425°F. Spread about ½ cup of refried beans in the bottom of the baking dish. Cover the beans with tortilla chips. Dollop more refried beans on top of the tortilla chips, top with some of the chicken mixture, and sprinkle with some of the cheese. Repeat the layers until you have used up all the chips (or the dish is completely full), ending with the cheese.

3. **BAKE THE NACHOS.** Bake the nachos in the preheated oven for 10 to 15 minutes, until the whole thing is heated through and the cheese is melted.

4. **GARNISH AND SERVE.** Scatter the jalapeño slices and olives over the top of the nachos. Dollop with sour cream, salsa, cilantro, and any other toppings you like. Serve immediately.

BAKED MEXICAN BEEF, BLACK BEAN, AND POLENTA CASSEROLE

Prep time: 15 MINUTES   *Cook time:* 35 MINUTES   *Serves:* 4

LEVEL 1

NUT-FREE
GLUTEN-FREE

EQUIPMENT
9-inch square baking dish, large skillet, spatula

Nonstick cooking spray

1 (18-ounce) package precooked polenta, sliced

Salt

Freshly ground black pepper

1 tablespoon vegetable oil

½ onion, diced

1 pound ground beef

2 tablespoons chili powder

1 tablespoon ground cumin

1 tablespoon paprika

1 (4-ounce) can diced green chiles

1 (14-ounce) can black beans, drained and rinsed

1 cup shredded cheese (I use a Mexican blend)

¼ cup sliced black olives

¼ cup chopped fresh cilantro, for garnish

This is a take on a traditional tamale pie, but it uses slices of precooked polenta as a base instead of a cornmeal dough topping. The fact that the polenta is already cooked makes it a great shortcut. This recipe is easy to change up, using different types of meat, cheese, and beans for variety.

1. **PREHEAT THE OVEN AND PREPARE THE PAN.** Preheat the oven to 350°F. Spray the baking dish with cooking spray.

2. **MAKE THE POLENTA LAYER.** Layer the polenta slices in the prepared baking dish, pressing them into the gaps to completely cover the bottom of the pan with an even layer. Season with salt and pepper. Bake in the preheated oven for 15 minutes.

3. **MAKE THE FILLING.** While the polenta layer bakes, in a large skillet over medium-high heat, heat the oil. Add the onion and cook, stirring, until softened, about 5 minutes. Add the beef and cook, stirring and breaking up the meat with a spatula, until thoroughly browned, about 8 minutes. Add the chili powder, cumin, and paprika and cook, stirring, for 1 more minute. Stir in the chiles and beans, and remove the skillet from the heat.

4. **ASSEMBLE THE CASSEROLE.** Spoon the meat mixture into the baking dish, and spread it in an even layer over the polenta. Top with the cheese, and sprinkle the chopped olives over the top.

5. **BAKE THE CASSEROLE AND SERVE.** Bake in the preheated oven until the cheese is melted and bubbling, 15 to 20 minutes. Serve hot, garnished with the cilantro.

STACKED CHICKEN ENCHILADAS

WITH SALSA VERDE

Prep time: 15 MINUTES   *Cook time:* 35 MINUTES   *Serves:* 6

LEVEL

NUT-FREE
GLUTEN-FREE

EQUIPMENT
9-inch square baking dish,
medium mixing bowl

Nonstick cooking spray

3 cups salsa verde

¾ cup sour cream, plus more
for garnish

12 (6-inch) corn tortillas

2½ cups shredded
cooked chicken

2½ cups shredded cheese
of your choice

Chopped olives, sliced
avocado, and chopped
cilantro, for garnish
(optional)

Enchiladas make a really satisfying and tasty meal.
This version is quick and easy to make because it uses
store-bought green salsa as a base for the sauce and
precooked chicken in the filling. You can use leftover
roasted or grilled chicken, or use a rotisserie chicken
from the supermarket.

1. PREHEAT THE OVEN AND PREPARE THE DISH. Preheat the oven
to 375°F. Spray the baking dish with cooking spray.

2. MAKE THE SAUCE. In a medium mixing bowl, stir together the
salsa verde and sour cream until well combined.

3. ASSEMBLE THE ENCHILADAS. Spread about one-third of the
salsa and sour cream mixture in the bottom of the prepared
baking dish. Arrange 4 tortillas in the bottom of the baking
dish, cutting them as needed, to cover the bottom of the dish
completely. Top with half of the chicken, half of the remaining
salsa mixture, and one-third of the cheese. Repeat with 4 more
tortillas, and add the remaining chicken, half of the remaining
salsa, and half of the remaining cheese. Continue to add layers
until you run out of ingredients, ending with the cheese.

4. BAKE THE ENCHILADAS AND SERVE. Bake in the preheated
oven for 30 to 35 minutes, until the cheese on top is lightly
browned and bubbling and the whole thing is heated through.
Let cool slightly before serving with dollops of sour cream and
additional garnishes as desired.

THREE-CHEESE AND SAUSAGE LASAGNA

Prep time: 30 MINUTES, PLUS 15 MINUTES TO COOL   *Cook time:* 1 HOUR 15 MINUTES   *Serves:* 6 TO 8

LEVEL 2

NUT-FREE

EQUIPMENT
Large saucepan, large mixing bowl, 9-by-13-inch baking dish, aluminum foil

FOR THE SAUCE

2 tablespoons olive oil

1 pound spicy or sweet Italian sausages, casings removed

1 small onion, diced

3 garlic cloves, minced

2 teaspoons dried oregano

1 (28-ounce) can crushed tomatoes

1 (14½-ounce) can diced tomatoes

Salt

Freshly ground black pepper

FOR THE FILLING

3 cups part-skim ricotta cheese

1½ cups shredded mozzarella cheese

¾ cup freshly grated Parmesan cheese

1 egg, lightly beaten

½ cup fresh basil leaves, finely chopped

½ teaspoon salt

¼ teaspoon freshly ground black pepper

Lasagna is a real crowd pleaser, and it makes great leftovers, too! No need to precook the noodles—simply layer them in the pan along with the other ingredients, and they cook to perfect tenderness in the sauce.

1. MAKE THE SAUCE. In a large saucepan over medium-high heat, heat the oil. Add the sausage, onion, garlic, and oregano and cook, stirring frequently, until the sausage is cooked through and the onion is softened, about 10 minutes. Add the crushed tomatoes and diced tomatoes, along with their juices, and bring to a boil. Lower the heat to medium-low, and simmer for 5 minutes. Season with salt and pepper.

2. MAKE THE FILLING. In a large mixing bowl, stir together the ricotta, mozzarella, Parmesan, egg, basil, salt, and pepper.

FOR ASSEMBLING

1 (8-ounce) package lasagna noodles (not "no-boil"), divided

3 cups shredded mozzarella cheese, divided

1 cup freshly grated Parmesan cheese, divided

Nonstick cooking spray

3. ASSEMBLE THE LASAGNA. Preheat the oven to 375°F. Spread 1¼ cups of sauce in the bottom of the baking dish. Arrange noodles in a single layer over the sauce (about 3 noodles, breaking as needed to fit). Dollop 1½ cups of filling over the noodles, and use the back of a spoon to spread it evenly over them. Sprinkle ¾ cup of mozzarella and ¼ cup of Parmesan over the filling. Make 3 more layers of sauce, noodles, filling, and cheese. Top with a final layer of noodles, the remaining sauce, and the remaining cheeses. Cover the lasagna with aluminum foil (spray the bottom of the foil with cooking spray first to prevent sticking).

4. BAKE THE LASAGNA AND SERVE. Bake in the preheated oven for 40 minutes. Then raise the temperature to 400°F, remove the foil, and bake for about 20 minutes more, until the cheese on top is puffed and golden brown and the sauce is bubbling. Remove from the oven and let cool for 15 minutes before serving.

CAULIFLOWER AND CHEESE PASTA BAKE

Prep time: 15 MINUTES   *Cook time:* 40 MINUTES   *Serves:* 6 TO 8

LEVEL

EQUIPMENT
Large pot, large mixing bowl, large skillet, 9-by-13-inch baking dish, small mixing bowl

12 ounces medium-size pasta (such as shells, rotini, or penne)

Salt

5 to 7 tablespoons olive oil, divided

1 large head cauliflower, cut into small florets, divided

2 tablespoons chopped fresh sage leaves

2 tablespoons capers, drained

3 garlic cloves, minced

Freshly ground black pepper

2 cups shredded fontina cheese

1 cup ricotta cheese

½ cup panko bread crumbs

6 tablespoons freshly grated Parmesan cheese

2 tablespoons pine nuts

2 tablespoons minced flat-leaf parsley

When cauliflower is roasted in the oven, it caramelizes, which is really just a fancy way of saying that it becomes sweet as it gets cooked—and that's what makes it irresistible. Combine that with cheese, some herbs, and perfectly cooked pasta, and you've got the makings of an excellent meal. You'll have plenty for leftovers, or you can freeze it for up to 3 months.

1. **COOK THE PASTA.** Cook the pasta in a large pot of salted water according to the package directions just until *al dente* (almost, but not completely tender—it will fully cook when you bake it.) Drain the pasta, and return it to the cooking pot or a large mixing bowl.

2. **SAUTÉ THE CAULIFLOWER.** In a large skillet over medium-high heat, heat 2 tablespoons of oil. Add half the cauliflower and cook, stirring occasionally, until it begins to brown, about 6 minutes. Add the sautéed cauliflower to the pasta, and cook the remaining cauliflower the same way before adding it to the pasta as well.

3. **ADD THE REMAINING INGREDIENTS.** Add the sage, capers, garlic, salt, and pepper to the pasta, and stir to combine. Add the fontina cheese, and stir to combine. Transfer half of the pasta mixture into the baking dish. Dollop the ricotta in spoonfuls on top of the pasta, distributing it evenly over the top. Spoon the remaining pasta mixture on top, and spread into an even layer.

4. **MAKE THE TOPPING.** In a small mixing bowl, stir together the bread crumbs, Parmesan cheese, pine nuts, and 1 tablespoon of olive oil. Scatter the mixture evenly over the top of the pasta.

5. **BAKE THE PASTA AND SERVE.** Bake in the preheated oven for 25 to 30 minutes, until the dish is thoroughly heated through and the topping is browned and crisp. Serve immediately, garnished with the parsley.

BAKED MAC AND CHEESE
WITH CRUNCHY TOPPING

Prep time: 10 MINUTES   *Cook time:* 40 MINUTES   *Serves:* 6

LEVEL

NUT-FREE

EQUIPMENT
Large pot, small mixing bowl, medium saucepan, 9-by-13-inch baking dish

FOR THE PASTA

8 ounces elbow macaroni

Salt

1 tablespoon unsalted butter

FOR THE TOPPING

⅔ cup panko bread crumbs

2 tablespoons unsalted butter, melted

¼ teaspoon salt

FOR THE SAUCE

¼ cup unsalted butter

⅓ cup all-purpose flour

3 cups (whole or low-fat) milk, warmed, divided

¾ teaspoon salt

½ teaspoon mustard powder

2 cups shredded sharp Cheddar cheese

1 cup shredded mozzarella or fontina cheese

Forget the boxed stuff—you haven't truly experienced mac and cheese until you make it from scratch. It is so much better! You can use just about any cheese you like, as long as it's not too mild in flavor and is a good melting cheese— like Cheddar, Gruyère, Swiss, or fontina.

1. **COOK THE PASTA.** Cook the macaroni in a large pot of salted water for about 1 minute less than the package directions (so it is *al dente*, almost but not completely tender). Drain the pasta well, and return it to the cooking pot. Toss with the butter.

2. **MAKE THE TOPPING.** In a small mixing bowl, stir together the bread crumbs, melted butter, and salt.

3. **PREHEAT THE OVEN AND MAKE THE SAUCE.** Preheat the oven to 350°F. In a medium saucepan over medium heat, melt the butter. Stir in the flour and cook, stirring, for 1 minute. While stirring, slowly add 1 cup of milk, making a smooth paste. Stir in the remaining milk until the mixture is smooth and well combined. Stir in the salt and mustard powder. Continue to cook, stirring constantly, until the sauce thickens, 6 to 8 minutes. Remove the pan from the heat and stir in the cheese.

4. **ASSEMBLE THE CASSEROLE.** Add the sauce to the buttered pasta in the pot, and stir to coat well. Transfer the mixture to the baking dish, and spread it into an even layer. Sprinkle the topping evenly over the top.

5. **BAKE THE CASSEROLE AND SERVE.** Bake in the preheated oven until the top is golden brown, about 25 minutes. Serve immediately.

CHEESY POTATO STACKS

Prep time: 20 MINUTES   *Cook time:* 45 MINUTES   *Makes:* 12 POTATO STACKS

LEVEL 1

NUT-FREE
GLUTEN-FREE

EQUIPMENT
Standard 12-cup muffin tin,
small microwave-safe bowl,
aluminum foil

Nonstick cooking spray

2 tablespoons
unsalted butter

2 garlic cloves, minced

½ cup heavy
(whipping) cream

1 tablespoon minced fresh
thyme leaves

½ teaspoon salt

¼ teaspoon freshly ground
black pepper

2 pounds potatoes, peeled
and cut into very thin
slices, divided

1 cup shredded Swiss,
Cheddar, or Gruyère
cheese, divided

If you love cheese and potatoes (and who doesn't?), you're going to adore these stacks of potato slices baked in rich cream and topped with lots of melty cheese. This will especially appeal to vegetarians or make a lovely side dish for any meat-filled meal.

1. PREHEAT THE OVEN AND PREPARE THE PAN. Preheat the oven to 350°F. Spray the wells of the muffin tin with cooking spray.

2. MAKE THE SAUCE. In a small, microwave-safe bowl, stir together the butter, garlic, cream, thyme, salt, and pepper. Heat in the microwave in 30-second intervals, stirring in between, until the butter is completely melted and the mixture is smooth.

3. ASSEMBLE THE STACKS. Stack the potato slices in the wells of the muffin tin, making stacks about halfway up the wells. Spoon 1 teaspoon of the cream mixture over each stack, then sprinkle half of the cheese over the stacks, dividing equally. Add the remaining potato slices, filling the wells to the top. Pour the remaining cream mixture over the potatoes, dividing equally.

4. BAKE THE STACKS AND SERVE. Cover the pan with aluminum foil, and bake in the preheated oven for 35 minutes. Remove the tin from the oven, remove the foil, and sprinkle the remaining cheese over the top. Bake, uncovered, until the potatoes are tender and the tops are golden brown, about 10 more minutes. Remove the tin from the oven and let stand for a few minutes before serving hot.

MASHED POTATO AND BEEF CASSEROLE

Prep time: 15 MINUTES, PLUS 15 MINUTES TO COOL   *Cook time:* 1 HOUR   *Serves:* 6

LEVEL

EQUIPMENT

Medium saucepan with lid, potato masher, large skillet with lid, spatula, 9-by-13-inch baking dish

FOR THE TOPPING

1½ pounds russet potatoes, peeled and cut into ½-inch dice

¼ cup (whole or low-fat) milk

¼ cup (½ stick) unsalted butter

¾ teaspoon salt

¼ teaspoon freshly ground black pepper

1 egg yolk

FOR THE FILLING

2 tablespoons vegetable oil

1 onion, diced

1½ pounds ground beef

1 teaspoon salt

½ teaspoon freshly ground black pepper

2 tablespoons all-purpose flour

1 cup chicken or beef broth

1 teaspoon Worcestershire sauce

1 cup frozen peas and carrots

This is comfort food at its finest. Buttery mashed potatoes form a luxurious topping for a mixture of seasoned ground beef. The filling is studded with peas and carrots, too, so it's a full meal in one dish.

1. MAKE THE TOPPING. Put the potatoes in a medium saucepan and fill with water to cover by about 1 inch. Cover and bring to a boil over high heat. Remove the lid, and lower the heat to medium-low. Simmer the potatoes until tender, 10 to 15 minutes. Drain the potatoes, then immediately return them to the saucepan and add the milk, butter, salt, and pepper. Mash with a potato masher or the back of a fork until the mixture is smooth. Add the egg yolk, and stir to mix well.

2. MAKE THE FILLING. Preheat the oven to 400°F. In a large skillet over medium-high heat, heat the oil. Add the onion and cook, stirring, until softened, about 5 minutes. Add the ground beef, salt, and pepper and cook, stirring and breaking up the meat with a spatula, until thoroughly browned, about 5 minutes. Sprinkle the flour over the meat and cook, stirring, for 1 minute more. Stir in the broth and Worcestershire sauce, and bring to a boil. Lower the heat, cover the skillet, and simmer until the sauce thickens a bit, about 10 minutes. Stir in the peas and carrots.

3. ASSEMBLE THE CASSEROLE. Transfer the meat mixture to the baking dish. Spoon the mashed potatoes on top, then spread them out into an even layer completely covering the meat.

4. BAKE THE CASSEROLE AND SERVE. Bake in the preheated oven until the potatoes are golden brown and the sauce is bubbling, about 25 minutes. Remove the pan from the oven and let cool for 10 to 15 minutes before serving.

THE CASSEROLE: YOUR NEW BEST FRIEND

Picture a lasagna—noodles lovingly layered with homemade sauce, spinach, cheese, and meat. This is comfort food at its finest, and it falls under the category of casserole. One-dish meals like this are found in all countries and all cultures around the world. In Greece, ground meat, eggplant, tomato sauce, and cheese are layered in flavorful *moussaka*. In France, home cooks make *cassoulet*—a hearty concoction of meats, sausages, and white beans simmered with garlic and spices and topped with a crunchy breadcrumb topping.

Casseroles really started to take off in the late 1880s when ovens became more commonplace in the average home kitchen. And they stayed popular because they taste wonderful, they can feed a crowd, they transport well, and they reheat nicely, making them great for any number of get-togethers or celebrations. Plus they can be as fancy or as humble as the ingredients you choose. So, embrace the casserole and you'll soon have an array of go-to recipes your family and friends will ask for again and again.

SAVORY BREAD PUDDING

Prep time: 10 MINUTES, PLUS 15 MINUTES TO SOAK   *Cook time:* 40 MINUTES   *Serves:* 8

LEVEL 1

NUT-FREE

EQUIPMENT
9-by-13-inch baking dish, medium skillet, large mixing bowl, whisk

1 tablespoon unsalted butter, plus more for greasing

1 onion, diced

4 garlic cloves, minced

8 eggs

1½ cups half-and-half

2 tablespoons Dijon mustard

1½ teaspoons salt

Pinch freshly ground black pepper

1-pound loaf stale French bread, cut into 1-inch dice

1 pound Canadian bacon, cut into ½-inch dice, divided

1½ cups shredded Gruyère cheese, divided

¼ cup finely grated Parmesan cheese, divided

Turn a loaf of stale bread into a breakfast fit for royalty by layering it with Canadian bacon, sautéed onions, and cheese and then baking it in a creamy egg custard. This dish makes a great breakfast, brunch, lunch, or dinner.

1. **PREHEAT THE OVEN AND PREPARE THE PAN.** Preheat the oven to 350°F. Grease the baking dish with butter.

2. **SAUTÉ THE ONION AND GARLIC.** In a medium skillet over medium-high heat, melt the butter. Add the onion and garlic and cook, stirring, until the onion is softened, about 5 minutes. Remove from the heat and let cool.

3. **MIX THE CUSTARD.** In a large mixing bowl, whisk together the eggs, half-and-half, mustard, salt, and pepper. Add the bread cubes, and stir to coat. Let the bread soak in the egg mixture for at least 15 minutes (you can refrigerate it overnight if you like).

4. **ASSEMBLE THE BREAD PUDDING.** Spread half of the soaked bread cubes in the prepared baking dish. Spoon half of the onion and garlic mixture on top. Add half of the bacon, then sprinkle half of each cheese over the top. Add the remaining bread cubes in a second layer, topping with the remaining onion, bacon, and cheese. Pour the remaining custard mixture over the top.

5. **BAKE THE BREAD PUDDING AND SERVE.** Bake in the preheated oven for about 35 minutes, until the custard is set and the top is golden brown. Serve immediately or let cool to room temperature before serving.

Tip

Don't have stale bread? Spread fresh bread cubes on a baking sheet and heat in a 350°F oven for 10 minutes.

CONVERSION TABLES

VOLUME EQUIVALENTS (LIQUID)

STANDARD	US STANDARD (OUNCES)	METRIC (APPROXIMATE)
2 TABLESPOONS	1 FL. OZ.	30 ML
¼ CUP	2 FL. OZ.	60 ML
½ CUP	4 FL. OZ.	120 ML
1 CUP	8 FL. OZ.	240 ML
1½ CUPS	12 FL. OZ.	355 ML
2 CUPS OR 1 PINT	16 FL. OZ.	475 ML
4 CUPS OR 1 QUART	32 FL. OZ.	1 L
1 GALLON	128 FL. OZ.	4 L

OVEN TEMPERATURES

FAHRENHEIT (F)	CELSIUS (C) (APPROXIMATE)
250°	120°
300°	150°
325°	165°
350°	180°
375°	190°
400°	200°
425°	220°
450°	230°

VOLUME EQUIVALENTS (DRY)

STANDARD	METRIC (APPROXIMATE)
⅛ TEASPOON	0.5 ML
¼ TEASPOON	1 ML
½ TEASPOON	2 ML
¾ TEASPOON	4 ML
1 TEASPOON	5 ML
1 TABLESPOON	15 ML
¼ CUP	59 ML
⅓ CUP	79 ML
½ CUP	118 ML
⅔ CUP	156 ML
¾ CUP	177 ML
1 CUP	235 ML
2 CUPS OR 1 PINT	475 ML
3 CUPS	700 ML
4 CUPS OR 1 QUART	1 L

WEIGHT EQUIVALENTS

STANDARD	METRIC (APPROXIMATE)
½ OUNCE	15 G
1 OUNCE	30 G
2 OUNCES	60 G
4 OUNCES	115 G
8 OUNCES	225 G
12 OUNCES	340 G
16 OUNCES OR 1 POUND	455 G

BAKING FOR SPECIFIC EVENTS

Bake Sale Bestsellers

Flourless Double Chocolate Cookies, 67
Cinnamon Pinwheel Cookies, 70
Candy Bar Cookies, 72
Whoopie Pies, 74
Raspberry Melt-Aways, 78
Lemon Bars, 81
Fudgiest Brownies, 84
Coffee-Toffee Blondies, 85
Chocolate Chip Cookies and Milk Cake, 96
Peanut Butter and Jelly Cupcakes, 98
Espresso-Mocha Cupcakes with
Buttercream Frosting, 100
Vanilla Confetti Cupcakes, 102
Campfire S'mores Baked in a Glass, 108
Strawberry Hand Pies, 116
Lemon Chess Pie, 126
Pistachio Blackberry Tart, 127
Key Lime Tart, 131
Chocolate-Cherry Black Forest Tart, 133
Chocolate-Hazelnut Tart, 136

Pep Rally Winners

Flourless Double Chocolate Cookies, 67
Candy Bar Cookies, 72
Coffee-Toffee Blondies, 85
Peanut Butter and Jelly Cupcakes, 98
Espresso-Mocha Cupcakes with
Buttercream Frosting, 100
Vanilla Confetti Cupcakes, 102

Study Session Fuel

Chocolate-Cherry Granola Bars, 82
Coffee-Toffee Blondies, 85
Espresso-Mocha Cupcakes with
Buttercream Frosting, 100
Olive Bread Twists, 145
Cheesy Straws, 146
Honey-Wheat Sesame Crackers, 147
Giant Soft Pretzels, 148
Pigs in Puffs, 150
Bacon-Cheddar Cheese Puffs, 152

Movie Night Munchies

Olive Bread Twists, 145
Cheesy Straws, 146
Giant Soft Pretzels, 148
Pigs in Puffs, 150
Bacon-Cheddar Cheese Puffs, 152
Pesto and Turkey Toaster Pastries, 158
Spanakopita Cups, 166
Classic Thin-Crust Pizza, 167
Sausage and Cheese Calzone, 170
Chicken Nachos, 174
Baked Mac and Cheese with
Crunchy Topping, 181

Game Night Delights

Cheesy Straws, 146
Giant Soft Pretzels, 148
Pigs in Puffs, 150
Bacon-Cheddar Cheese Puffs, 152
Pesto and Turkey Toaster Pastries, 158
Classic Thin-Crust Pizza, 167
Sausage and Cheese Calzone, 170
Chicken Nachos, 174

Party Pleasers

Candy Bar Cookies, 72
Whoopie Pies, 74
Homemade Macarons, 76
Raspberry Melt-Aways, 78
Lemon Bars, 81
Red Velvet Cheesecake Bars, 83
Angel Food Cake with Raspberry Glaze, 88
Double-Layer Carrot Cake with
Cream Cheese Frosting, 90

Cream-Filled Chocolate Layer Cake, 92
Lemon Pudding Cake, 95
Chocolate Chip Cookies and Milk Cake, 96
Peanut Butter and Jelly Cupcakes, 98
Espresso-Mocha Cupcakes with
Buttercream Frosting, 100
Vanilla Confetti Cupcakes, 102
Pineapple Dump Cake with
Coconut Frosting, 104
Blueberry-Swirl Cheesecake, 106
Campfire S'mores Baked in a Glass, 108
Strawberry Shortcake in a Jar, 111
Deep Dish Peach and Blackberry Pie, 114
Apple Pie with Cinnamon-
Streusel Topping, 120
Banana Cream Pie, 122
Chocolate-Peanut Butter Cup Pie, 123
Kiwi and Strawberry Tart with
Vanilla Pastry Cream, 124
Lemon Chess Pie, 126
Pistachio-Blackberry Tart, 127
Upside-Down Caramel Apple Tart, 129
Key Lime Tart, 131
Chocolate-Cherry Black Forest Tart, 133
Chocolate-Hazelnut Tart, 136

Sleepover Slam Dunks

Glazed Lemon Scones, 45
Blueberry Yogurt Muffins, 46
Oatmeal-Chocolate Chip Muffins, 47
Peanut Butter–Filled Banana Muffins, 48
Gingerbread Coffee Cake in a Mug, 50
Pumpkin Spice Breakfast Bread Pudding, 55
Maple-Pecan Morning Bun
Breakfast Cake, 63
Strawberry Hand Pies, 116

RESOURCES

Classes

SUR LA TABLE

www.surlatable.com

This cookware chain offers hands-on cooking and baking classes for kids and teens in their stores, which are located around the country.

CRAFTSY

www.craftsy.com

This website offers online baking courses for every level. You'll find classes on cookie, cake, pie, and bread baking as well as classes on cookie, cake, and cupcake decorating.

Blogs

17 AND BAKING

www.17andbaking.com

This baking blog was started by a Seattle teenager. She's older now, but her blog still features lots of fun and doable recipes written with younger bakers in mind.

CHOCOLATE COVERED KATIE

www.chocolatecoveredkatie.com

This is another baking blog that was started by a teenage baker. Katie focuses on "healthy dessert recipes," but don't worry, they are also delicious and beautiful!

INDEX

ACKNOWLEDGMENTS

I am deeply grateful to all the young bakers and cooks out there experimenting in their own kitchens, reading recipe blogs and cookbooks, watching cooking shows and Youtube cooking videos, taking cooking classes, and learning about cooking from family and friends. Because of you, all of our tomorrows will be more delicious.

ABOUT THE AUTHOR

Robin Donovan is a food writer, recipe developer, and author of numerous cookbooks, including the bestselling *Campfire Cuisine*, *Deceptively Easy Desserts*, and *Dutch Oven Obsession*. She lives in Berkeley, California, and blogs about easy recipes for people who love food at www.TwoLazyGourmets.com.

CPSIA information can be obtained
at www.ICGtesting.com
Printed in the USA
BVHW060735151118
533117BV00019BA/1242/P